F!
THAT!
DON'T
SHRINK

DR. TAMARA R. GRIFFIN

Disclaimer: This book is not designed to diagnose or replace the professional assessment of a clinician. For more in-depth information, counseling or therapy regarding mental health and/or other concerns, please contact your primary physician, therapist or other mental health clinician.. If you feel you are experiencing a mental health or medical emergency, put this book down immediately and call 911, your medical or mental health provider and/or go to your local hospital.

DEDICATION

F! That Don't Shrink! is dedicated to life! It's dedicated to the change that grew out of my necessity to live and to be authentic to me and all my parts...the good, and the ...well, not so good!

I was fighting to live and to exist in a way that would not cause me to sacrifice or compromise myself anymore. There's a distinct difference between compromise and sacrifice. Compromise is something that you can live with, whereas sacrifice means that you give up a part of yourself. Both can be good; however, when sacrifice becomes detrimental to our spirit and soul, it is at the point that you must decide whether you want to live or die.

F! That! I chose to LIVE MY LIFE!

If we are not living authentic to who we are, then we'll spend the rest of our lives dying to live.

TABLE OF CONTENTS

ACKNOWLEDGEMENTS

EVOL. I've never met a spirit, a soul quite like you! I thought I knew what love was, but then you showed up, and it was in that very moment that I realized that everything I knew about love was founded on some superficial experience based on society's misguided and unhealthy messages of love. But you—you loved me on a soul level, spiritual level, cellular level, energetical level, biochemical level! Our love is Divine, something beyond ourselves. How in sync we are? I have never felt so free to be who I am in my life the way I am with you! Thank you for your strength and your vulnerability! Thank you for your transparency through the challenging times! Each tear we cried together helped us to become that which we are. Thank you so much for loving me, for me, without condition, without limits! Thank you so much for being the safe space in which I can reside my heart without fear! I have found my sanctuary with you in this life and the next! I rest well in you! You are my life partner, my 24, my 3, my twin flame. To thee, I commit until! We have no ending, for we transcend this space and time...LOVE!

Janice, girl where do I begin? You know, you really should get paid to be a therapist!! You're good at that "-ish!" No really, thank you for letting me spill at the tea! Thank you for listening to me rambling and babble as I made sense of life. You never once judged me. You always had a good word that would get me right together! See, when you didn't think I was, I was listening! LOL! Most importantly, thank you for always reminding me that I didn't have to shrink! We been doing this—what, about 20 years now—and even though we're no longer the 20-something year olds sitting around waiting to count the days, we still look good gurl! LOL! By the way, I think we finally found the answer to the question, so get ready for the cover of Essence, Ebony and Jet! So, here's to us!

A LOVE LETTER TO MY BELOVED

My Beloved,

I know how it feels to shrink! I know from first-hand experience the devastation and damage shrinking can cause. I also know the shame, the trauma, and the pain that results from shrinking! I know how difficult and challenging it can be to face yourself and admit that you've shrunk. I know it feels damn near impossible to try to pick up your "-ish" and move on with your life. But I also know that if we don't, we die! We die mentally, emotionally, spiritually, socially, financially, and physically - including death. But here's the great new, As difficult and challenging as it may be, it's not impossible! If I can do it, you can too! YOU CAN TOO!

No more excuses, My Beloved! It's time to grow up and glow up! No longer shall we allow ourselves to shrink! No longer will we be an active participant in allowing ourselves to shrink. So wipe the tears from your eyes, ease the worry and doubt from your mind, erase the hurt and pain from your heart and let go of the resentment and disappointment that has been weighing you down! Scream it out! Shout it out! Just let it go!

Now, keep in mind that just because we make a concerted effort to prevent shrinkage, doesn't mean it won't ever happen because it just might. So, if by chance we find ourselves in a shrinking situation, it's ok! However, what's not ok is allowing ourselves to stay in it, throw a pity party, and use it as an excuse for why life sucks! From this moment forth, that is no longer acceptable because we now have the knowledge, skills, and tools to be able to do something about!

We have to put on our big girl panties or favorite pair of drawers and forgive it, feel it, face it, forget it, find it, and get yo fancy unapologetic self right together and say F*uk it! I got this because you got this! We, My Beloved, got this!

So from this day forward, now and forever more, shall we say with the power and authority that hath been bestowed upon us...F! That! We won't shrink!

CHAPTER 1
ME AND MY F! THAT! ATTITUDE!

About nine years ago, I published a book entitled *Live Inspired Feel Empowered...*yup, LIFE! The book was about...yup, you guessed it ...LIFE; my life in particular. In this book, I shared and recounted many experiences that I had gone through. I relived each one as if I were experiencing them all again. During this process, I felt vulnerable! I felt afraid. I was embarrassed and ashamed that I had allowed myself to experience such abuse. I wondered what people would think now that they knew my story. Would they look at me differently? Would they whisper when I walk by? Nevertheless, I knew I had to share my story. I am so very thankful that I did because I know that my story helped to empower so many other women and girls. It helped to change their lives! Countless women have called me or sent emails, letters, or texts to let me know just how much *Live Inspired Feel Empowered* helped them to become the woman that they've always wanted to be. It is in those moments that I realize that everything I went through—from the failed relationship until publishing the book—was all worth it!

After I wrote the book, everything was good! I did the work! I began to live inspired and feel empowered! Everything was all good! That's all I had to do to continue living the good life, right? Wrong! Who was I kidding?

Although LIFE was an absolutely amazing and necessary book to get me through that particular time and space in my journey, it could not have prepared me for the new journey that I was on. Like the saying goes, new levels, new devils. This space in my life would bring on newer and tougher challenges...challenges that would inevitably cause me to question myself in ways I never had before. This space would create rifts with those close to me! This space would allow me to experience LIFE in a brand new and unapologetic way. I was truly not prepared for that way, but I was ready to face it.

One morning, I was sitting on my patio, sipping coffee and taking in the beautiful view of the sunrise and Frenchman Mountains. As I sat there, I began to think about my life. On the surface, things seemed to be going pretty well, all things considered. But as I began to dip a little deeper beneath the surface layer, I began to wonder if I was truly happy and satisfied with who I was and where I was. Was my life headed in the direction I wanted? My answer was no. As I sat there in almost disbelief, I wondered how that could be?

Shocked by my brutally honest answer, I knew it was time to face my -ish! And so the work began...

I began to dig a little deeper, trying to figure out what this revelation really meant? As I continued to peel back the layers, I realized that I had the career of my dreams and had speaking engagements lined up across the country. Also, I was in the process of opening my Vegas Chick Fit studio, and I was married and living in one of the most fabulous cities in the world--so fabulous that over 1.1 million people visit it per year.

What more could I want? It was simple! I wanted authenticity! I want to be me! Now, was that too much to ask? Hell, I thought I was being me. But, when I dug deep down inside and faced my -ish, I wasn't. I was too busy living for *them* and I was not living for me. What happened?

Disappointment began to settle in...

Had I sacrificed myself to the point that I no longer recognize myself?

My opinions?

My thoughts?

My style?

My hair?

My smile?

My voice?

My core?

My everything???

As I sat there now *completely* devastated, I realized that all this time I had been living in this absolutely beautiful glass house that society, intergenerational patterns, them, they, and others, had built for me. Over time, the atmospheric pressure has chipped away, causing cracks to the foundation. Apparently, the cracks had gone unnoticed for some time. If a crack is not repaired quickly, the stress placed on the ends of the crack almost guarantees that the crack will continue to spread along the same line, much like faults that produce earthquakes. What started off as a small chip in my foundation became a huge crack. And before I knew it, I had a giant mess on my hands!

So, here I am yet again in this same space of embarrassment and shame as I gather myself and thoughts in preparation to write this book! But it's not like I haven't done this, right? (Or at least that's what I tell myself.) Nevertheless, I can't help but to wonder what will "they" think. Because, after all, I am the same woman who wrote a book about how to Live Inspired and Feel Empowered. I am the same woman who did the necessary work to heal! That was me, right? ME?! But as I sit here writing this introduction, I extend myself grace, for I have realized that LIFE, living inspired and feeling empowered, is not a one-time event! It's a LIFEstyle! It's a constant journey! And even within that, there is constant growth, re-evaluation, dismantling and rebuilding of self.

As long as we live, there will always be "stuff" that we have to deal with, layers that we have to peel back in order to continue living inspired and feeling empowered...in order to reside in our authenticity. Because if we do not, *we shrink!* We become a hollowed former shell of ourselves. We shrink into the abyss of nothingness... I'm here to tell you, My Beloved, F! that! whatever you do, *don't shrink!* No matter how hard it is, we must not allow ourselves to shrink!

Where does the courage come from to walk away from it all and begin to live? Where do we find the strength to say F! That! and step out boldly and courageously into our authenticity? How do we become bold enough to forego the societal norms and traditions, to live out loud and on purpose? How do we live LIFE on our terms without sacrificing too much of ourselves? If you're like me, you've asked these questions a million times. Well guess what, I've finally found out! Now don't get me wrong, I'm not saying that I have found the answer! What I am saying is that I found a way to learn how to say, "F! That!" and refuse to shrink!

Over the next few sentences, paragraphs, pages, and chapters, I am hoping that you find strength and purpose. I am hoping that you will connect with you on an authentic level, touching the deepest part of your soul that will inspire you to say, "F! That! I refuse to shrink!" This book will help you, (as it did me) take an in-depth look into our lives. It will shine a reflection that will reach into the depths of your soul! This book will make you face your -ish! Yup…I know it's not easy! As a matter of fact, it's tough, but you won't be doing anything that I haven't done and still continue to do! Besides, you're not alone! I'm walking along this journey with you!

On the following pages, you will find my voice, my story! You will also find inspirational quotes and my "Morning Cup of F! That! with Coffee," tips and tools that I have used and continue to use. You will even find yourself! Don't be surprised if you don't necessarily like what you see. It's ok! Extend yourself grace! Be loving, gentle, and kind. Whatever you do, don't give up! Cry! Scream! Yell! Do whatever else you need to do! But from this day forth, F! That!

Morning Cup of F! That! with Coffee…

Thank You, Jesus, for reminding me how important it is to be true to MYSELF—no matter what that is, and/or if it changes from day to day! Thank You for giving me the strength to do what I believe and feel is right for ME, even when others disagree and/or do not understand! Most of us live a life by the design of others—spouses, kids, partners, parents, bosses, friends, enemies, society, culture, religion, etc. When we do, we allow them to dictate OUR path. As a result, we end up conflicted because we're trying to do something that is so unnatural to our spirits. We're denying our true selves, so we fight and struggle internally, remaining miserable until we begin doing what we know is right for us. My Beloved, we cannot live the life that others want us to live! We have to follow our guide, our inner voice/gut feeling, no matter how much others may try to prevent us from doing so. Having the courage to be bold enough to step out on faith and move through fear, judgment, and criticism is how it begins. Have enough belief in YOURSELF to know and do what's best for YOU, even if you sometimes have to do it alone! Remember you're never *truly* alone! God is *always* with us! Those who genuinely love us will encourage us, even if they don't understand. And if they don't, F'em! Our joy comes first and that begins by being true to self! Honor yourself TODAY, persevere your authenticity, and refuse to shrink!

CHAPTER NAME 2
SO...WHAT DOES IT MEAN TO SHRINK?

Shrink [SHriNGk]
VERB

shrinks (third person present) **shrank** (past tense) **shrunk** (past participle)
shrunken (past participle) **shrinking (**present participle)
 1. become or make smaller in size or amount; contract or cause to
  contract:
 2. move back or away, especially because of fear
 3. to become reduced in amount or value; dwindle
 4. to show reluctance; hesitate:

Simply put, to shrink is to diminish your value and worth for the sake of others; to sacrifice yourself to the point that you no longer recognize that person that you've become. You become reluctant or hesitant to share your voice because you fear that others may not accept you, or you fear it may cause too much controversy within your relationships. You dim your light and play the background so that your spouse, partner, friend, boss, co-worker doesn't feel like you're trying to outshine them.

If you have done any of the aforementioned things to accommodate others continuously to a point that it leaves you with feeling of frustration, anger, or sadness, then yes, you my Beloved shrank, have shrunken or you are currently shrinking!

Why Do We Shrink?

For as long as I can remember, I have always been different from my peers. I was born with it. I *knew* I was special. I had this certain *je ne sais quoi*! I was the creative, right brain type. I was the kid who would rally the neighbor kids and get them to buy into whatever I was doing at the time; whether it was riding our bikes, creating a music group, baking brownies, playing kickball, having a yard sale, or listening to me give some kind of kid speech! I truly believed that the world was mine. I could do or be anything I wanted to, because I had this special connect to the world.

However, as I got older—middle school into adulthood—life around me began to happen. I was being taught to view the world in a way that felt very unnatural. It felt contradictory to my spirit. As I fruitlessly tried to navigate a new worldview that was so different from mine, I began to lose sight of who I was. My *je ne sais quoi* began to be overshadowed by the desire to fit in. I began to shrink just so I could fit in to this new worldview that I was being introduced to. I shrank to be noticed. I shrank so my friends would feel better. I shrank so a boy would like me. I shrank so my boss would not feel threatened. I shrank because I felt like I no longer had "it." I didn't deserve "it"—whatever "it" was at the time. As a result, I became painfully shy, and paralyzed with insecurity and fear, which left me in a constant state of self-doubt and self-criticism. I began searching for validation from others because I no longer felt that being me was enough. I no longer felt this deep sense of myself. I no longer felt a special connection to the world.

Now how did this happen? How did I go from being sure of myself to becoming smaller than life? It's as if I reached a certain age and the beauty and magic of life were gone!

The harsh reality is that the larger society doesn't really care and people can be cruel. Even those who love us and may have the best intentions for us— at least in their minds—can sometimes create an unhealthy environment for us. We are also bombarded with unhealthy marketing and imagery about how we should live, what success looks like, and what we aspire to. We receive these messages from a variety of sources—family, friends, partners, media, society, religion—and if we're not very careful, these messages become footprints embedded in consciousness that end up changing the trajectory of our lives forever. They become deep-seated, unconscious controllers that cause use to shrink because we have been conditioned to look at the world in a way that contradicts who we are.

We Shrink for a Variety of Reasons

In order to begin growing into the person that you want to become, you first have to understand what's causing you to shrink. You must identify obstacles to growth and empowerment that are hidden deep within your subconscious. It is time to identify those obstacles so that you can consciously and actively deal with them.

How do we do this?

This process begins by first taking an honest look into the very depths of our souls to understand who we are and what our intrinsic and extrinsic influences are. We also must factor in our cultural, gender, social, religious/spiritual, values, morals and sexual thoughts, beliefs and behaviors, and the roles each plays in helping to shape our perception of self. Moreover, we must understand how all of this shows up within the Dimensions of Wellness. All these things are embedded within the blueprint of our life. Peeling back these layers is critical to overcoming obstacles that contribute to shrinking and serve as a barrier to growth and empowerment.

"Figure out who you are separate from your family, {society, et al.}, and the man or woman you're in a relationship with. Find who you are in this world, and what you need to feel good alone. I think that's the most important thing in life. Find a sense of self because with that, you can do anything else." -Angelina Jolie, Cosmopolitan Magazine

The Bullshit Society Sold Us

Society has colored this beautiful picture of what life is and how it should be. It hangs in front of us like a priceless work of art hanging in a museum. The moment we see this picture, we become enchanted with the vibrant colors, the details, and the intricacies of the lines. We spend the rest of our lives trying to recreate this perfect picture. However, the moment we color outside the lines, our perfect masterpiece becomes flawed and useless— at least according to society.

As a little girl, I grew up listening to fairytales such as Cinderella, Snow White, and The Princess and the Pea. In each of these stories, the main character, a young woman, was portrayed as a helpless damsel in distress that needed to be saved by a young man (in Snow White's case, it was seven dwarfs). In each of these stories, these young women needed the assistance of a young man in order to be complete.

Even a girl's toy choices are heavily centered around being a wife and a mother. Barbie, baby dolls, and Easy Bake Ovens, did not give little girls many choices regarding their socialization. From the moment a woman finds out the sex of the baby, we are gendered. Little girls get pink and little boys get blue. From that moment on, our lives become a pink-a-palooza and we become bombarded with all things *"girly!"*

Couple this message with the heavily value-laden, moralistic societal messages of the 50's and 60's which indicated that the American dream is for a young woman to make herself presentable enough to find a husband to marry, move into the white house with the cute little picket fence, have two and a half kids and get a dog.

So let me get this right—the path to wholeness and empowerment for a woman requires being saved by a man, getting married, and having children, a white picket fence, and a dog?

Hmmm...

Nowhere in any of these messages do we find a story of empowerment. Nowhere in any of these messages do we see the young woman who graduates high school, goes off to college, becomes a successful executive who maybe (or maybe not) decides to have kids and get married. Nowhere do we find a message that indicates that a young woman can be complete, healthy, and whole without the assistance of, or being saved by, a man.

What type of bull -ish is this? It's no wonder many women, both young and old, (including myself) struggle with their identity and clarity of their roles as women. We spend our lives shrinking trying to fit neatly into this one-size-fits-all model.

I know that I have shrunk trying to be something that I was not and am not! I have spent many years of my life in a space that had completely devoured my spirit and diminished my self-esteem, all because I tried to embody a societal script that was not written for me. It took me years to learn that this script was not written for me. It took me even longer to gain the courage to toss that script to the wayside and to finally write one that was perfectly imperfect for me because I'm definitely not Cinderella, Snow White, or the Princess and the Pea!

<u>Super Woman Persona</u>

When I was in high school, Karyn White sang a song called "I'm Not Your Superwoman." I loved the song! I sang it all the time. Although I knew the words to the song, I really didn't know the words to the song. I did not truly understand the "superwoman" struggle that she sang about. All I knew about being superwoman was that she was this mystical comic book character turned TV show character played by Linda Carter and every week she would wrangle up bad guys with her lasso of truth, magical sword, and indestructible bracelets, and fly away in her invisible jet.

By nature, women are nurturers. Women have been taught to take care of everyone and everything with little consideration for our own needs and wants. Even when we don't feel like it or have the strength, we are expected to keep going despite what's going on because after all, we are a "superwoman."

Yes! We have rightfully earned the title of "superwoman" because we have the uncanny ability to meet all the demands from others that have been placed on our lives, but by trying to live up to this superwoman persona, we have unconsciously allowed our needs and wants to fall by the wayside. Unfortunately, by the time we get around to caring for ourselves, we are so burnt out that we don't have enough energy left. We try relentlessly to live up to an image that creates all sorts of internal chaos and dysfunction. Meanwhile, everyone and everything around us continues thriving while we're barely surviving.

Society, family, friends, co-workers, partners, spouses, kids, pastors, etc. will have you all F*cked up! Trying to be everything to everyone is not possible because in the midst of it all, you shrink into the abyss of nothingness. We become lost and/or irrelevant to everyone and everything around us.

As flattering as it is to be all things to everyone, we need to lovingly shift our focus and attention back to meeting our own needs first. "Is this selfish?" you ask. Absolutely not! It is what I like to refer to as the *law of self-preservation*! During a flight, the flight attendant states that if there happens to be a loss of cabin pressure during the flight, that passengers must first securely fasten their own masks before assisting others. "First, securely fasten your masks before assisting others" is the exact approach we need to take for our lives. The bottom line is that if we are not whole, healthy, happy individuals, then we are not in a position to be of support or assistance to anyone else. We have to empower ourselves with the knowledge, tools, and skills to prevent ourselves from shrinking.

Guilt

Guilt is a cognitive and/or an emotional experience that occurs when we believe that we have compromised our integrity. Guilt is also a powerful tool that can be used to manipulate someone's behavior and is something that is strongly linked with the need for external approval.

Most people have been conditioned to feel guilt. This guilt usually comes from family, friends, spouses, partners, society, religion, or culture. We learned consciously (or unconsciously) to feel guilty for thinking or acting in a certain way, or when do not give in to how others think we should behave.

It is very draining and distressing living with a constant feeling of guilt. Continuing to focus on how guilty you feel will keep you feeling anxious and confused. When you are focused on the feelings of guilt, it doesn't matter what you do, you're going to continue feeling guilty because that's what you're concentrating on. Your mind continuously replays the "should've, would've, could've" game over and over again. This ultimately causes more guilt, which causes you to shrink.

Living with guilt also stops you from making the most effective and efficient decisions. In other words, you'll end up making unhealthy decisions simply because you're reacting to feelings of guilt.

Man...do I ever know about guilt! I have carried around guilt like an extra weight on my shoulders! It's no wonder why my back hurt all the time! LOL! But seriously, guilt is heavy, and it weighed me down for years. What's interesting about it is that for me, I felt guilt not so much for doing other people wrong or for disappointing other people--I felt guilty for disappointing *me*. I felt guilty for not being true to myself and THAT guilt caused me to shrink. What's even worse is that I continued to do it to myself time and time again! No matter how many times I said I wouldn't, I did, and that would just create more guilt. One of the most distressing things in life is to feel guilty about disappointing ourselves; however, most of the time we're too busy focusing on everything and everyone else that we don't even realize it. Or we do realize it, so that's why we're focused on everything and everyone else. Either way, it's not healthy because when we don't face our -ish we ultimately end up shrinking to the point of nothingness.

The Need for Approval

Who doesn't want to be accepted, especially by a loved one? Social media has magnified this need for approval because now you have a way to compare your life to others (or at least the life that they portray). If you're a Facebook Fanatic, Instagram Insomniac, or Twitter Tweaker like me, then you're constantly surfing and scrolling, reading statuses and posts. Sometimes, I get so overwhelmed by the posts of folks in the hospital looking pitiful, half-naked girls, and other overly dramatic posts, all vying for "likes." On the flip side of things, I also feel incredibly dazed looking at all the absolutely amazing things that folks are doing, while my life completely sucks at times. Then, I begin to question myself and immediately find myself seeking some sort of approval. Just like most people, I, too, have struggled with the need for approval, especially from my partner. I wanted my partners to validate me and when they did not, I questioned and doubted myself big time almost to the point that I did not feel like I could make a decision or move forward without their approval. I wanted them to approve of everything I did, from my outfit to my career, until one day I realized how totally unrealistic and unhealthy to live for someone else's approval. I had to realize that my approval for the outfit I was wearing, the career moves I had chosen, or the life I was living was good enough! I had to realize that even if no one else approved, that I could go one and still be ok being me! I am Dr. TaMara and I approve this message!

Approval, acceptance, and validation is something that we all desire. As children, we were taught to seek approval from our parents for the things we did or said. When we did or said something good, they gave us praise, which is directly linked to acceptance. When we did or said something "bad," the praise was withheld and met with disapproval. Because human beings develop such a strong desire to be accepted and receive praise, we may sometimes shrink to please other people. However, if we are not careful, this desire to receive approval can turn into a lifetime of consciously and unconsciously seeking approval from others for the things we say and do. This is dangerous because we may engage in unhealthy behaviors and unhealthy relationships trying to seek approval and validation from others. It tears you apart and sends you on a vicious cycle of self-destruction.

For example, there may be something that you feel, want to do, or want to say, but your loved one disapproves. Therefore, in order to avoid receiving disapproval, you decide to go along with whatever he or she says or however he or she feels.

Over time, this behavior results in shrinking because you've chosen to conform to a way of life that feels very unnatural to you. This creates internal conflict, which can result in anxiety, depression, frustration, or resentment of your partner, because you are not being authentic to how you feel and/or who you are.

Morning Cup of F! That! with Coffee...
I am grateful for self- acceptance! Ever since I can remember, I have always been a little different! I have always done my own thing when it comes to fashion, hairstyles, decorating, and even the way I think and process information. I've never really followed trends and nothing about me is conservative. I've never tried to be different: it's just who I am! Was I

teased, criticized, laughed at, and talked about? Of course! But I'm so thankful that I had parents who accepted, encouraged, and nurtured my individuality! They allowed me to explore and discover me. Often, we try so hard to fit neatly into an ideal that society has created. Anything outside that ideal is abnormal, threatening, or unacceptable. It's so unfortunate because we stifle people's ability to grow and maximize potential based on ignorance and fear. As a result, we have people succumbing to substance use and abuse, low self-esteem, stress, depression, violence, and death. My Beloved, let's not allow society to dictate OUR normal. No longer do we have to fit neatly into anybody's ideal of who we are or should be! It's time to start accepting others and ourselves for who we are and who they are. We are all perfectly imperfect just the way we are! So, let's make some time today to look in the mirror and say, "I accept me! I love me! And I am ok just the way I am!"

Embarrassment

Embarrassment killed many dreams. For years, I lived under the burden of embarrassment. I would talk myself out of many things because I was too embarrassed by what others would think. I allowed this feeling to have way too much weight in my life. As a result, I have missed out on so many opportunities. I have also utilized my gifts. When I was younger, I had a beautiful singing voice. I wanted to be in the entertainment industry, but I was always too embarrassed to sing in front of people, so I never really pursued it. I allowed embarrassment to steal my dream.

We've all done something that totally embarrassed the crap out of us. Most of the time, we bounce back from that cringe-worthy moment. However, depending on the nature of the context of the embarrassing experience, it may cause us to shrink and withdraw from certain situations, people, social settings, or conversations.

Embarrassment is another emotion closely associated with guilt and shame. It is dictated by a disconnect between how we feel we should respond or act in public and how society feels we should respond or act in public. We are most likely to be embarrassed when we believe we have not lived up to what society dictates.

Our embarrassment is influenced by the negative evaluations we presume individuals will have of us if we mess up. This presumption (real or perceived) may make us feel self-conscious, exposed, awkward, or vulnerable. The experience of embarrassment alerts you of your failure to behave according to certain social standards. This threatens the beliefs you hold concerning how others evaluate you as well as the ways in which you evaluate yourself. And because embarrassment is such a public emotion, whenever we do something that we consider embarrassing, it can diminish our self-esteem which increases the likelihood of withdrawing and/or not engaging in activities that will encourage public interaction. This causes us to shrink into a space of insecurity and self-defeat.

<u>Cultural Norms</u>

Cultural norms are the standards we live by. They are the shared expectations and rules that guide behavior of people within social groups. Cultural norms are found in all societies but vary widely among various groups and populations. Cultural norms are learned and reinforced from parents, friends, teachers, and others while growing up. As you were growing up, you learned certain things "norms"--about your culture. These beliefs were taken as truth and you've never taken the time to think about or question whether these cultural norms held any relevance, or how much they may have influenced your adult life. Whether you are aware of it or not, cultural norms affect virtually every part of daily life, and often become so routine that you're are unaware of the significant role they play in determining how people dress, act, and interact with others.

Generally speaking, the members of a society judge one another when a person breaks a cultural norm. This is especially true when people behave in a manner that violates a taboo, which is a norm that is so strongly upheld that breaching it results in extreme judgment and shaming from others.

A cultural norm that I learned growing up as a young Black girl was that wearing a dress to church was something that all prim and proper "good girls" do. I also learned that "good girls" don't do this, they don't do that and my gosh (gasping and clutching my pearls) they never, not ever, did this! I began to think, "Well, damn! Do they ever have fun because it certainly seems like "good girls" don't do anything?" As I got older, I realized that this particular "good girl" cultural norm no longer was applicable to my life. Nevertheless, I felt that if I did not continue subscribed to this "norm" that I somehow would no longer be considered normal. So here I am with a struggle between "staying true" to an antiquated cultural norm or being considered <u>abnormal</u> because I make the difficult decision to embrace my new normal outside of traditional cultural norms. Because no one wants to stick out like a sore thumb or be considered abnormal, we shrink and succumb to those cultural norms against our best interest, even if it almost kills us--and sometimes it does!

Morning Cup of F! That! with Coffee...

Thank You, Jesus, that I am NOT normal! What the heck is "normal" anyway? Normal is a bunch of BS; a "standard" that society has deemed acceptable to make others feel comfortable while isolating anything that is different. Normal is a statistical average that ignores the beautiful diversity of life, a very narrow path that fails to allow for any deviation. Normal polices anything that doesn't fit perfectly into societal, familial, cultural, spiritual, or political expectations...norms. These norms convince people that they are emotionally unbalanced because of their lifestyle choices that dare to be different. But the crazy thing about it is that these so-called norms change all the time based on any given number of reasons. Trying to keep up and fit in with norms only creates internal disharmony and chaos. That's why it's so much better to just be yourself! My Beloved, we have to begin to challenge normal! The construct of normal breeds pathology by which others try to diagnose. Who wants to fall within or abide by a guideline that creates a space for non-tolerance, judgement, and violence? Who wants to be a clone of society's fear of life! Who wants to be normal when there are so many beautiful colors to life? Who wants to be normal when normal is based on the fallacy of reality. Who wants to be normal when it's just so much easier to be you! Not this chick!! F! being normal! I'm not really interested in normal! It's not my goal! I dare to be different! I dare to live a life that is not confined to beliefs, judgment, stigma that is held in place by elitist privilege folks who lack the gumption to challenge conventional notions. I refuse to blend into the monotony of life by allowing normal to neutralize my creativity and box in my exceptionality. Trust and believe this life ain't for the faint at heart! But I'd rather live life unrefined than to be sucked into the stereotypical and safe path of normal! Y'all can keep your normal! That's just not me...

"-ism"s

As a dark-skinned Black woman, I have certainly experienced my fair share of "-isms": racism, sexism, colorism, classism, erotic capitalism, etc. To have an "-ism" be the first thing a person sees when you enter the room or to be unfairly treated because of someone else's discomfort and/experience with an "-ism" is very disheartening. It's truly difficult to live in a world that defines you this way. Living in the shadow of an "-ism" or multiple "-isms" is difficult to navigate. It can create significant duress, which can cause us to shrink.

An "-ism" can be described as a thought or belief about a person or group of people that creates an unjustifiable divide between a person or a group of people. "-Isms" are essentially created by the dominant group to soothe their need for psychological security and comfort.

"-Isms" create a social, systemic and institutionalized oppression work to establish a "defined norm" or standard of rightness under which a person or group of people are unfairly judged and/or treated. "-Isms" of all kinds can have a profoundly harmful and lasting effect on our personalities through constant conditioning and association with beliefs that have been wrongly attributed to a person or groups of people.

If we align our very identity with an "-ism" within, we become bombarded by societal beliefs until that "-isms" become lodged into our personalities, our perceptions, and begins to define how we see ourselves. The way in which we experience and internalize "-isms" play a contributing factor in our overall health and well-being. "-Isms" create systems of oppression, contribute to a deep-rooted sense of hate, and reinforce shame, stigma, secrecy, and guilt, which contributes the way we shrink. Women, especially Black women experience the brunt of "-isms" including racism, sexism, classism, erotic capitalism, etc. This intersectionality of gender, race, sex, class, and capitalism produces and perpetuates systems of oppression and domination. A mind that flooded with an endless cycle of "-isms" cannot experience the beauty of life because it is so focused on the unhealthy images projected by "-isms."

If I had to embody any particular "-ism", it would be Eclecticism. According to Wikipedia, an eclecticism is *a conceptual approach that does not hold rigidly to a single paradigm or set of assumptions, but instead draws upon multiple theories, styles, or ideas to gain complementary insights into a subject, without conventions or rules dictating how or which theories were combined.* I'm *totally* unconventional, and I *definitely do not* hold rigidly to a single paradigm or set of assumptions. I take a funky, eclectic, bohemian, dope approach to living, while keeping in mind that life is fluid and no particular set of rules can dictate that at any time!

The Four Letter Word: Love

It took me some time to learn the true meaning of *love*. Even though I had loved before, I never really understood how true love works. It was not until I was in my 40s that I finally understood love and how it works. And to be completely transparent, I am still learning all about the beauty of love, not just with a partner, but with myself.

This 4-letter word, how powerful it is! Love is one of the world's most sought-after emotions. One of the most frequently misunderstood and misused terms! An action verb, often imitated by some cheap, knock-off version. Conditionally unconditional, but TRUE love perfects all! Love is patient in our impatience. Love never dies; it just changes from one form to another. I just had to learn to recognize it!

Right or wrong, good or bad, we learned how to love from our parents, whether they played and active parts in our lives growing up or not. If our parents were present and active, we learned how to express love and receive love. If they weren't present or active, we learned that perhaps we were undeserving of love.

What we learn about love from our parents becomes the foundation of how we will experience love with ourselves, partners, and the world around us. If we received healthier messages about love, we tend to have a healthier experience with relationships. The more unhealthy experiences and messages we received about love, the more likely we are to engage in riskier behaviors, even if it means sacrificing ourselves. This can be a dangerous place to be in because it sends the message that we are willing to do *whatever* to be loved.

Of course, there are times when we must be willing to make a sacrifice for love. Sacrificing for someone you love may help you show them you care and may even make you feel loved. However, if you find yourself *always* being the one who sacrifices, or feel forced to make a sacrifice, then you may want to re-evaluate the relationship. When we sacrifice too much of ourselves, it can become exhausting and begin to wear on you emotionally, mentally, physically, socially, and spiritually. That exhaustion will turn into bitterness and resentment towards your partner and yourself because you've sacrificed too much of yourself, and now, you've shrunken to the point that you have nothing left to give!

Morning Cup of F! That! with Coffee...
Today, I am so grateful that even in a crazy world, I still believe in love! This 4-letter word is so powerful! Love is one of the world's most sought-after emotions and one of the most frequently misunderstood and misused terms! Love is an action verb often imitated by some cheap knock-off version. Conditionally unconditional, but yet, TRUE love perfects all! Love is patient in our impatience. Love never dies; it just changes from one form to another, and we have to learn to recognize its different forms. I believe in love's miraculous healing powers that can heal a shattered and scattered broken heart. For love does not fail us: we fail love, belittle love, and mistreat love when it does not become what we so selfishly desire. We turn our backs on love, blaming it for our random transgressions and indiscretions. Love cannot be bought or sold; manipulated or contrived; or held onto tightly out of fear. Love is freedom to be just as we are! It soars

with an Angel's glow--on the wings of love we grow! I believe in love and its ability to transform lives as I have seen it at work in mine. I strive to walk within love's ecstatic state, beyond the world of limitations into the world of boundlessness! But--in order to ascend, for love to work--we must not be afraid to risk being vulnerable enough to open our hearts, forgive, let go and let God! For He is LOVE! HE...IS...LOVE! And the greatest of these...is LOVE!! F! everything else, I'm all about LOVE!

Morning Cup of F! That! with Coffee...

Love is real! To experience it is surreal! People will do some crazy things all for the sake of (or in the name of) love. Over the years, I have loved and lost, and loved and lost again! Each time I loved, I believed it was real, regardless of the outcome. What I took away from each dance with love was intense, raw, and real! Not once did I ever question love. I questioned myself because I was the common denominator in all of the experiences. And you know what? I figured out that I had this love thing all wrong. I was living in the illusion of love. What I learned is that we really don't understand the true essence of love. Love is not the superficial emotion that Hollywood has sold us for years! It's not some feeling that makes our heart skip a beat! It's not a verb that we base someone's actions on. Here's the heavy part...love is definitely not comfortable! Contrary to popular belief, love is very uncomfortable! Ask Jesus! He died on the cross all because He loved! He suffered all because He loved us! He dealt with the hate and judgment of others all because He loved us! The essence of love is the ability to endure! It's strength! It's the ability to prevail against all odds! It's the power to overcome and RISE again! That's love! It's an undying, unstoppable energy that is transferred from one to another. My Beloved, we can't transfer something we do not truly embody. At best, we're transferring some watered-down misconception that we've mistaken for love. To truly experience love in all its essence, we have to first embody love for ourselves. If we don't, we merely transfer our -ish to someone else, get mad at them, and/or end up hurt. The funny part is that we then swear that love does not exist or that it's not real. Well, my Beloved, it's not that love is not real or does not exist, we just failed to give it to **ourselves first**! What we can't find in ourselves, we damn sure can't find in others! I believe in love and its ability to transform lives as I have seen it at work in mine. I want to lay to rest that whole fallacy about falling "in love"...it doesn't exist! Besides, who wants to "fall" into anything? F! That! I want to *live* love 365 days a year! There's nothing else I'd rather do than love! And...ahhh! It feels so good!

<u>Obligation</u>

"If you are living out of a sense of obligation, you are slave." ~Wayne Dyer

An obligation is something you feel compelled to do. Usually when we think of the word obligation, the following terms come to mind: "owe," "expect," "burden," "have to," "duty," "forced," "legally bound," etc., which in my mind are not necessarily great feelings to carry.

From an early age, we are taught the importance of obligation. We are obligated to society, family, friends, spouses, partners, teachers, employers, culture, and race. The sense of obligation keeps us committed to things, people, and places that we may no longer want to be committed to.

When we feel obliged to something or someone we no longer want to be obligated to, we begin to experience resentment for being obligated to respond, behave, act, or think a certain way. Eventually, we begin to become rebellious. Being hindered from freely expressing ourselves in a way that feels authentic and real becomes emotionally draining, mentally exhausting, and spiritually overwhelming. It can also cause feelings of frustration, stress, anxiety, depression, and even physical symptoms such as fatigue and headaches. But because we feel this overwhelming sense of responsibility, we stay stuck in the situation which creates duality and conflict causing us to shrink.

"Your only obligation in any lifetime is to be true to yourself." ~ Richard Bach

"You have no obligation under the sun other than to discover your real needs, to fulfill them, and to rejoice in doing so." ~François Rabelais

<u>Intergenerational/ Cross-generational Patterns</u>

Passed down from generation to generation, unhealthy negative patterns, behaviors, and beliefs are like virus, replicating and spreading from one family member to the other, infecting our thought pattern and becoming deep-rooted within our subconscious mind.

As young girls, we learned about ourselves from what we were taught and exposed to or not exposed to by our mothers, who learned from her mother, who learned from her mother, and so on. If our mother did not know how to be empowered, it would have been next to impossible for her to teach her daughter how to be an empowered woman. This is not an attempt to place blame on your mother for anything but rather to help identify some of your behavior patterns that may to contribute to the very circumstances you face today. And because you haven't been taught and don't know any differently, you will continue to shrink until you identify the dangerous, negative cyclical behaviors and commit to changing them.

"You are much more powerful today than the old thoughts, beliefs and behaviors that were programmed and absorbed during your childhood." ~Wayne Dyer

You are not obligated to fulfill the destiny dictated to you through kinship. You can decide at this very moment to break the negative cycle by reprogramming your thoughts, beliefs, and behaviors. By doing so, you begin to chart a new course, you change destiny for yourself and future generations of women within your family. Give yourself permission to identify each old negative pattern, behavior, and/or belief, examine it, make peace with it, and release it to the universe as your first step toward empowerment/ healing.

Morning Cup of F! That! with Coffee...
Thank You, Jesus, for helping me to break the cycle! "Grandma and them" and "momma and them" will have you all F*ed up! They had a way of doing things that worked for them. Over the years, they passed down these intergenerational patterns, thoughts, beliefs and behaviors to us. Some of these things were very helpful or healthy, while others were, well...not so much! And it's the not so much that is harmful to us. The interesting part about all of this is that we never questioned grandma, momma, or "them" about why they did what they did. We've just accepted what was passed down as gospel! And most of the time, we just continued on in the same vein--good or bad--as grandma, momma and them without even knowing and understanding why. The only answer we have to explain our thoughts, beliefs, and behaviors is...that's how I was raised. But is that good enough? Our failure to ask questions or challenge these intergenerational patterns, thoughts, beliefs and/or behaviors leaves us without a true sense of self, which is essential for our identity and sense of authenticity. What worked for grandma, momma and them, may not work for us! When we were kids, we did not have a choice but as adults, we most certainly do! My Beloved, it's time to break the cycle! It's time to create your own path! It's time to do what works for you! F! sticking to those old antiquated intergenerational patterns, thoughts, beliefs and behaviors! I absolutely refuse to stay in bondage and repeat the negative, unhealthy cycle and continue to fail generation after generation! It begins with us! So shall I pass you a hammer? 1...2...3--break that cycle!!

Low Self-Esteem

"If I didn't define myself for myself, I would be crunched into other people's fantasies for me and eaten alive." ~ Audre Lorde

The gateway to disempowerment, low self-esteem can be an obstacle to loving ourselves. If we don't love or even like ourselves, how can we believe that we deserve better? How could we ever position ourselves for greatness? We can't.

Self-Esteem is powered by self-acceptance. When we don't accept ourselves, we lack self-esteem. We also tend to place ourselves at risk because we don't care enough to believe we can do or demand any better. Low self-esteem usually manifest itself as self-defeating behaviors, lack of confidence, and lack of trust in oneself – all blocks to becoming and living an empowered lifestyle. When we lack self-esteem, we allow ourselves to be used and abuse seeking that which we believe is missing. Alternatively, we find comfort in sex, drugs, risky behaviors, and other unhealthy compulsions.

Another effect of low self-esteem is false sense of self with a super inflated self-esteem. In this case, we fool ourselves into believing that we have high self-esteem when actually it is just overcompensating for that which we lack or disapprove. And to protect ourselves or to seek acceptance and approval from the outside world, we create images and schemes of grandeur to "keep up" or to "fit in." Because we fear that our peers and/ or loved ones may find an unacceptable trait, disapprove, or find us less than desirable, we become this character in an effort to divert their attention from finding out who we really are. But when we become someone or something other than who we are, we are no longer true to ourselves. There begins the battle of duality between the true self and the ego, because we have in essence said that who we are is not good enough, so we create an alternate reality in an effort to be accepted, approved, and loved.

At various points in my life, I have suffered from low self-esteem. I did not feel worthy. I questioned whether I was good enough, smart enough, talented enough, pretty enough, if he loved me enough and even if I loved *myself* enough and because of this, I shrank. Talking about a deep, dark place! I pretty much spiraled out of control and before I knew it, I was barely hanging on to the edge of life, like barely! But God! Even though I had shrunk and even in the midst of the darkness, there was a glimmer of hope! When I tell you that I held onto that glimmer hope like my life depended on it, because it did, I was slowly able to learn how to accept and love myself again. Through therapy, digging deep, facing my -ish, and thorough, meaningful, and authentic self-work, my self-esteem increased.

Now, that's not to say that some days or moments I don't still struggle; I just have tools in place to handle it more effectively.

"You find love in quotation marks here because when someone truly loves you, they accept you just as you are at that very moment, without conditions, limitations, or faultfinding."
~Unknown

When you truly love yourself, you think enough of yourself not to place yourself in harm's way. You think enough of yourself to put yourself *first*. You think enough of yourself to know that you deserve *the best* and will accept nothing less! And when you don't, you shrink!

Low Self-Efficacy

Low self-efficacy and low self-esteem are interrelated. Self-efficacy is an essential element of loving yourself first. Self-efficacy is a belief in your abilities to produce your desired effect in any situation. Self-efficacy affects every area of our lives. It can determine how we feel, think, and behave. It also can have an impact on our level of motivation, quality of functioning, resilience to adversity and vulnerability to stress and depression.

There are several factors that affect and/or influence our self-efficacy: transitional experiences, social situations, physiological factors (i.e. "butterflies in the stomach), and unfounded perceptions (i.e. how we may be perceived by others or how we perceive other's successes, familial relationships, sense of personal agency, or peer influences).

Our sense of self-efficacy plays a major role in how you set goals, approach tasks, handle challenges, and overcome obstacles. When we have high self-efficacy, we believe that we can do whatever we put our mind to. We believe that we are in control of our own lives, that our own actions and decisions shape our lives. We have low self-efficacy, we tend to believe that situations are beyond our capabilities, focus on personal failings and negative outcomes, and/or lack confidence in personal abilities. We shrink because we see our lives as outside of our control.

Using my story of lacking self-esteem from above, although I was lacking self-esteem, I still had high self-efficacy. I still had enough hope and belief that I could pull myself out of the situation. Even though I did not necessarily know how, somewhere deep, DEEP down inside I knew I could--and not only that, I wanted to! I just had to learn how, and thankfully I did!

<u>Fear</u>

"Our fear can develop through direct experience or indirectly through social observation of other's experiences." ~Unknown

When I was younger, like most kids, I was pretty fearless. I was a risk-taker. I would try almost anything. I guess that saying, "God protects babies and fools," really applied to me because looking back, some of the things that I tried were downright foolish. The only thing I do remember being extremely afraid of were dogs. I'm not sure how that particular fear developed. I do not remember having an experience with a dog that would justify the fear. However, I do know that my mother did not particularly care for dogs, so perhaps in my mind that translated into a learned fear, or perhaps the trauma of an experience was so intense that I buried it in the back of my brain and have yet to recover the experience.

As I got older and began to experience life, I believe many of my fears were (and are) grounded in direct personal experiences. Even though I work diligently to try not to allow fear to take root within my spirit, I must admit that I have been guilty of allowing my fears to creep in and prevent me from accomplishing some things. However, in those moments when it does, I honor it very briefly and try to move forward and do it, despite my fear(s).

There are many things we fear: fear of failure, fear of success, fear of losing, fear of your partner cheating, fear of being vulnerable, fear of losing control. I could go on forever naming fears. Fear is a natural human emotion--in fact, it's one of the most powerful emotions in life. It can affect the decisions you make, the actions you take, and the outcomes you achieve. Fear is so debilitating. It keeps us stagnant and stuck by creating a barrier that prevents us from moving forward. Fear is at the crux of our negative, self-defeating thoughts that keep us immobilized and keeps us from experience life to its fullest. Two words that often guide our fear is "What if?" As a result, we create the worst scenario that could arise out of the "What if?" in our minds.

Fear can disguise itself as many things: anger, depression, anxiety, health issues, disgust, sadness, pain, hyperactivity, etc. Fear can prevent us from forming relationships and/or destroy the relationships that we have. It can lead to engaging in risky behaviors that can cause us to shrink away from the path of growth, success, change, and fulfillment.

"We gain strength, and courage, and confidence by each experience in which we really stop to look fear in the face...we must do that which we think we cannot." ~Eleanor Roosevelt

Morning Cup of F! That! with Coffee....

I'm so grateful that I've learned to use my fear as fuel. At times, I have allowed my fears to prevent me from doing things I really wanted to do and things I knew I should've done. As a result, I've missed sooooo many wonderful opportunities and experiences. I also missed out on some amazing people because of fear. Fear can be debilitating. It keeps us stuck and stagnant by disguising itself as many things such as: stress, loneliness, depression, worry, anxiety, etc. Fear is so good that it even appears in the form of a friend, a partner, a parent, a spouse, or a family member. Fear is one of the best techniques used by satan to prevent us from living, taking chances, enjoying life, and doing God's work. If we're afraid of something, we're less likely to do it. Now, of course, it's natural to wonder about the unknown, but to allow our fears to paralyze us is to prevent us from moving forward to becoming all we are meant to be. My Beloved, it's time to face our fears. Square up, look your fears in the face and, "say it with your chest" F! you, {insert fear here}!" Continue naming each and every one! Tell your fears to "pack yo' -ish and get out! I no longer will allow you to stop me from living my life as I choose to, or from fulfilling my God-given Purpose!" Y'all know that God did not give us a spirit of fear, but of power, love, and a sound mind, right? We shall move forth in love, allowing faith and hope to be our guide. Oh, and one last thing--moving forth in love does not meaning doing everything or anything that "they" approve of! Moving forth in love means that you honor your needs, wants, and desires first! That doesn't mean you don't love "them;" it just means you love yourself more and enough not to be miserable and controlled by fear!

Questioning Our Decisions

"A double minded man is unstable in all his ways." ~ James 1:8, King James Version (KJV)

Decision-making is an essential part of life. Every decision we make has the propensity to affect our life--positively or negatively, which is why it is essential to develop healthy decision-making skills.

Often the causes of indecisiveness or lack of proper decision-making skills are more mental than physical and are deeply rooted in the mind as a result of low self-esteem, low self-efficacy, bad relationships, poor self-image, a history of abuse, stress, and many other factors.

"No perfect decision exists. Going back and forth can block you from going ahead." When you decide to take a risk, you get better at the process and learn what happens when you make leaps. Confidence grows with action." ~Steve Mensing, Author

The art of decision-making lies in our ability to make a balanced decision with minimal risk and maximized opportunity for growth. Because life hinges on the capacity to make safe sound decisions, the inability to make rational decisions may have a much more profound impact on our lives, making us more susceptible to engaging in unhealthy risky behaviors.

Common sense, wisdom, experience, confidence, and trust in ourselves are what empower us to make responsible decisions. If we do not make decisions, we cannot have our wants and/or needs met, have rewarding experiences and/or vitally enriching lives. To live fully, we must embrace decisions with open hearts as an opportunity for growth. We must be willing to move beyond fear to empowerment by learning to trust in our ability to make healthier decisions.

Morning Cup of F! That! with Coffee...
Thank You, Jesus, for keeping me as I grow in my capacity to make decisions! It's said that Jesus watches over babies and fools. Well, I know for certain that it must be true because man...I have made some crazy decisions. I have gotten myself into some situations that only a baby or fool would get into! The only way I survived is simply because He kept me! You see the process of keeping is two-fold. God does His part, but we also have a part to do! Our part is to learn and grow from our situations. It's to become wise and discerning. When we fail to learn our lesson, we end up in the same ole crazy -ish over and over again. And then we wonder why God "let" this happen. Uhm...its not God or anyone else, it's us! We have to stop blaming our random foolishness on others...God included. We have to learn to put our big girl panties on and big boy drawers on and become accountable for our -ish! You see society doesn't teach us accountability. It teaches us to point the finger at everything and everyone else except ourselves. What kind of -ish is that? Oh! It's the kind of -ish that stinks! It's the kind of -ish that fools only ourselves and oh yeah it's the kind of -ish otherwise known as a false perception of self. My Beloved! It's time to grow the up and start making decisions that reflect wisdom and maturity. When we are young we speak and do as children. F that! I don't have time for childish decisions because I'm not a child anymore

Self-defeating Thoughts

"The most common way people give up their power is by thinking they don't have any."
~Alice Walker

Morning Cup of F! That! with Coffee...
When I was in high school, I adopted the mantra "expect the worst, but hope for the best." As I look back now, that had to be the dumbest -ish ever! Like why would anyone want to expect the worst? Why would anyone want to draw that negativity to themselves knowingly? That's crazy! What's even crazier is that I had the unmitigated gall to wonder why all these negative things were happening to me. It never crossed my childish mind that the reason I was dealing with a lot of BS and receiving the worst is that "I" expected it…Duh! It's the basic law of attraction. Whatever we put out into the atmosphere is what we're likely to receive. So, I was only getting what I expected…THE WORST! Whew! Thank God I grew up! As I have grown and experienced life, I've come to realize that I AM responsible for my thoughts and energy--my perspective--which I put out into the atmosphere. I draw unto myself those people, situations, and experiences, and I choose to draw love, light, peace, and positivity! My Beloved, we have the power over perspective! When the power of the mind, law of attraction, positive intention, and positive energy meet, our perspective on life, people, situations, and experiences, become beautiful! It's insane to intentionally draw negative people, situations, and experiences to ourselves all because of our perspective. F! That! Life is too short to spend with the worst! I'm purposefully and intentionally moving with positive perspective! I'm kicking "worst" out! It can't live here! So, pack yo' -ish and get out! You're absolutely not welcomed here anymore! Goodbye!

The author John Allen so eloquently stated, *"A man's mind may be likened to a garden, which may be intelligently cultivated or allowed to run wild; but whether cultivated or neglected, it must, and will, bring forth. If no useful seeds are put into it, then an abundance of useless weed-seeds will fall therein, and will continue to produce their kind."*

Our mind is extremely powerful! Whatever we think, we eventually become. If we think positive thoughts, we tend to lead a more positive life. If we think negatively, we tend to experience the negative side of life. So, you might be thinking, "If it's that easy, why don't we always think positive thoughts?" Well, that's much easier said than done. At any given moment, something can happen, our lives are thrown into a tailspin, and we don't exactly know what to think. Our thought process can become a defining point for the rest of our lives.

Another way self-defeating thoughts help us shrink is through the negative thoughts that we believe about ourselves. Any thought that you engage in that is self-sabotaging distracts you from your goals, and when those uninvited and unwelcome thoughts creep into your mind, it can be tough to resist them. When you're in the midst of a negative and repetitive pattern of self-defeating thoughts, it can be tough to see any alternatives and it can begin to have an unhealthy impact on your life.

Simply having a self-defeating thought doesn't necessarily mean that you're going to shrink, because it's natural to have those thoughts from time to time. The context that it takes in shaping our life makes the difference. When self-defeating thoughts begins to become repetitive and significantly interfere with the quality of your life, then it's an issue.

Hurtful Words

A wise person once said, *"There are two things you can't take back; words and a speeding bullet."* Once either has been released into the universe, there is great potential for death. It is so important to think before you speak and to choose your words wisely. If there is nothing else that I have learned over the years, it is that there is truly the power of life and death in the tongue. We can speak success or defeat over our lives based on the words we choose. If we choose to speak hate, we inadvertently bring more hate to our lives; if we speak love into lives, we'll experience more love. Hurtful words linger on in our mind, affecting our ability to make healthy decisions, thus putting us at increasing risk. When we have been told something repeatedly, it eventually becomes our reality. It becomes who we are, and once these things become part of subconscious and even consciousness, we begin to manifest a death of our spirit by words.

Think about how many times you've been told, "you're this" or "you're that," you're not good enough or smart enough." Initially, you may have not given in to this negativity; however, if this is something that has been continuously repeated, eventually you may start to think, "...hey, maybe there is some truth to this. You begin to shrink because you start to doubt yourself and eventually spiral into a negative pattern of unhealthy behaviors.

Morning Cup of F! That! with Coffee...
Words have power! Nothing would ever convince me of exactly how true this was until I died a thousand times at the words of my ex-husband! This man's words would cut like shards of glass, sting like a scorpion, and stab with hurt and pain. His words were so piercing that over time, I actually began to believe all the vile words he said to me and about me. It was during that period in our marriage that I really embodied the phrase, "death and life are in the power of the tongue." Whoever said, "sticks and stones may break my bones, but words will never hurt me..." was full of -ish!! Words hurt!! Man, words are like speeding bullets--once they come out, they cannot be taken back! The damage is already done! And even though you

may apologize, the words still leave footprints forever embedded in the person's heart. Apologies become empty like hollow hearts. Unfortunately, often we just talk without regards to what comes out of our mouths. We say things because we're upset, angry, hurt or in the midst of an argument/disagreement without regards to the potential damage or lasting impact it may have on our lives, other's lives and our relationships. We seem to forget or acknowledge that words hurt just as much, if not more, than physical pain, leaving lasting scars that can be difficult to heal. Words are very powerful! The words we speak (positive or negative) are manifested in our lives. Therefore, I try to choose my words very carefully. My Beloved, like the old folks used to tell us when we were kids, "watch yo' mouth!" F! That! It's not acceptable to pop off and say whatever you want to say in the heat of the moment, especially to those you say you love! We are in control of the words we choose to speak! So...what words will you choose today? What will you speak into your life? Let us pray that we always learn to think before we speak, choose our words wisely, choose words that are life-giving and that our tongues always be with grace (and love), seasoned with salt, that we may know how we ought to answer everyone. TODAY, I speak Divine Blessings and supernatural Favor over our lives!

Religion

Historically, religious organizations have been the foundation of the community, a vehicle for dissemination of information, and a conduit for providing social services for their congregants and the surrounding community. Religious organizations are a place that people trust and turn to in their time of need for peace, healing, and support. Most people would agree that religion can cause more good than harm; however, there are times when the beliefs, doctrine, by-laws, or leadership can be more harmful than helpful.

Religious beliefs and doctrine creates a specific framework in which we must live. Any time we step outside the boundaries of that framework, it creates a discrepancy because we've failed to do what our religious beliefs and doctrine has taught us to do. As a result, we shrink and struggle with how to reconcile what we may feel within our spirit to be true and right for us, versus what we have been taught by our religion. This internal struggle breeds hatred, bitterness, and resentment towards ourselves and others because in our spirit we know what's right for us yet religious indoctrination condemns us and tells us that it's wrong. This causes us to stay in a situation that is not healthy for us. Maybe it is detrimental to our well-being.

Growing up in a Christian home, divorce was not an option. Couples stayed together and stuck it out for better or for worse, right? That's pretty much what I did, to the detriment of sacrificing myself and some of my relationships with my family members. The crazy part about all this is that from the outside looking in, we appeared to be the perfect couple. We were perceived to have a model marriage, and many of our friends and colleagues stated that they envied our relationship and wanted to know what our secret to having such a happy marriage was. And why not? He was a well-decorated military officer making six figures, the life of the party, well dressed, and to top it off, he had a "Johns Hopkins University alumni trophy wife" on his arm. Perception was a smokescreen because people had no idea of the personal hell I was living in. I was very depressed and unhappy! I had been fed a bitter taste of love and marriage that lingered on like the foul stench of death.

To Love Again

For I'd rather sell myself into slavery than to ever fall in love again
for least I'd live than be tormented by the cost of affection
the price is far too great not even your soul can indemnify
offering of sacrament
peace of mind is the donation
the celebration for the revocation of self
I hate a love that hates me back
and in fact I'd rather stab myself a thousand times with a serrated edge
for at least I'd know in time the wounds would heal
and I'd feel so much better than before
I can't ignore
how acidulous, atrocious, and deceitful love is
bitter
the taste that lingers
like the foul decaying stench of death
lain like a lifeless corpse
a victim of love
our reminder of how absolute the feeling can be
to love or not to love is the question
the answer is painstakingly brutal
and unrelentingly honest
tell me, can you can't handle the truth
love ...I hate you too

©2006 TaMara Dillard (Dr. TaMara Griffin)

Here I am in the relationship with this man--my husband--and I'm bitter! I'm resentful! I'm dying, figuratively and damn literally! This was the man that was supposed to love me, take care of me, protect me, but all he did was hurt me. I was suffering mentally, emotionally, spiritually, socially, and physically! I was dying! It was so bad that I knew I had to get out because if I didn't, one of us was going to die! It was at that point I knew this marriage had to end because one, I am too much of a coward to kill myself, and two, black and white stripes do not look good on me (nor does orange)! Although I knew I had to get out because everything in my Spirit told me to, I still stayed. Because, after all, *"God does not smile on divorce." "You won't be blessed if you leave your husband." "For better, for worse, through sickness and health, 'til death do you part...blah, blah, blah, blah."* So now, I'm in this marriage trying to reconcile my religious teachings with what my Spirit is telling me. In the meantime, I'm shrinking, struggling, and fighting. I'm fighting with myself! I'm fighting with my religion. I'm fighting to stay alive! One day, my Spirit spoke to me and said, "Enough is enough!" From that moment on, I gathered myself together, and created a plan. I left my husband, and I left my religion and I haven't looked back since!

There is a difference between having a personal relationship with God and being buried head-deep in organized religious dogma and spiritual ignorance. Religious beliefs, bylaws and indoctrination can create unhealthy stressors, even setting up negative intergenerational patterns of abuse, trauma, and internalized abuse, which can make it difficult for people to heal. Religious trauma can be difficult to see because it is camouflaged by fear-based messages of sin and going to hell if you don't subscribe to the belief system of the religion.

Religion can also divide insiders from outsiders, saints from sinners, creating an invisible divide that should not exist when we will not tolerate religious ideologies that are different from ours. It happens when certain religions or denominations start believing that the teaching and morals of their own religion are superior than any other religion and/or denomination. It also happens when we condemn others who are engaged in "sins" that are not *our* "sins." But all have sinned and fallen short" ...but yeah, I won't go there though!

Religion has also been used to dominate, control, and coerce people. It has been used to justify racism, sexism, violence, hatred, killing, and so much more. As a result, many people have been misled by religious indoctrination. There is nothing more toxic to the soul or dangerous to our development as a person that believes in something that is wrong, misguided, or outdated.

Often, many religious organizations have become power- and money-hungry, man-made institutions, just like for-profit corporations. And like any corporation, to survive and grow a religion must find a way to build power and wealth. Many religious leaders target on their congregants by "selling" faith, preying on their members weaknesses and using judgmental dogma to shame members who can't afford "blessings" because they can't or just aren't paying tithes. Additionally, the imbalance of power and differentiation in treatment between male and female clergy helps to contribute to the shaming messages that female members receive. Hypocrisy of the leadership preaching one thing but actively doing another creates an unhealthy culture of silence that opens a space for abuse. Everyone from the choir stand to the backdoor knows that "certain" things are going on, but it's swept under the rug. The unfortunate thing about this is that many young women and men suffer at the hand of the leadership. This abuse of power can contribute to an increased risk for depression, anger, substance abuse, self-harming, or engaging in risky behaviors, all of which make people shrink.

Morning Cup of F! That! with Coffee...
Thank You, Jesus, for our **RELATIONSHIP!** Religion almost killed me! Like many of you, I grew up under a certain belief or religious system. I went to church! I went to vacation bible school and youth fellowship. I served on the "usher" board. I sung in the choir and even sang a few solos. At the time, I believed the doctrine, by-laws, Pastor, etc. that were in place. I never questioned them until I got much older and I realized how much religion played a role in my delusions, shaming, disempowerment, and abuse from my previous marriage.

In the same way, religion has contributed to many others unhealthy beliefs, attitudes, behaviors, violence, and even death. We have been taught that the church and its religion is the place where we're supposed to go when we need to be fed spiritually, socially, emotionally, mentally, and physically. It's the place where we're supposed to go when we're sick and in need of a healing! It's the place where we're supposed to go when we need to gather in His Name and commune with other saints. It's supposed to be the place where like-minded folks are all working towards the same goal. I often wonder if this is still the case, or have churches become so religiously righteous, yet so heavenly hurtful that they are no longer any earthly good?

The church isn't what it used to be, or is it? Now, check it out...I'm not knocking religion and the church, but then again, maybe I am. One thing for sure is that I am challenging the church, and I am pushing back on religion because man's interpretation and implementation of the doctrine and bylaws keep people stagnant, hurt, and, confused. I'm talking about how humans in leadership abuse power, prey on the weak, and sell Jesus for their own selfish gain. I'm talking about losing souls to hypocrisy, shame, and guilt disguised as control, blame, and condemnation. I'm talking about the fashion shows, saints fighting, Facebook praising, cliqued up congregational members, untouchable clergy surrounded by security, and cult-like behavior that will have you throwing up your church signs and reppin' your set. Oh, and I just love it when we're condemned to hell because of our sins, but their sins are excused because they're different than ours?

Well, Thank God man does not have a heaven or hell to put me in! And here's a little FYI--the same hell you're putting me in, is the EXACT same one you'll be in for your transgressions. Ain't no levels to this -ish! F! religion! It will have you F*ed up every time! That's why it's so important to have the RELATIONSHIP, because it's the relationship and the BELIEF in Him, NOT the religion, that saves us! So y'all can keep your religion! I'd rather have my relationship any day! I'd rather represent Him than the dogmatic, ever-changing doctrine and bylaws of religion and man! I'm real church representing Him out here in these streets! Not the doctrine, not the bylaw, and certainly not the man! Now...pass the collection plate. I'm taking up a love offering for the building fund! HA!

<u>Shame</u>

"We do not feel worthy because of the shame that we have experienced throughout the course of our lives. Our sense of worthiness is an important piece that gives us access to love and acceptance of ourselves. In order to begin to develop a sense of worthiness, we must understand the creation of shame and begin to address it." ~ Dr. TaMara

"Shame on you!" I'm sure growing up many of us have heard this phrase from our family, loved ones, or whomever wanted to teach us a *lesson,* or prevent us from engaging in some sort of *undesirable* behavior. They never stopped to think about the negative and unhealthy impact that shaming us would have on our lives. The footprints embedded in our subconscious and conscious mind have contributed to our self-esteem and self-worth.

Shame is about judgement, fear, secrecy, and silence. It is a very hurtful and harmful emotion that can result from the comparison of self to societal ideals, behaviors, and standards. Shame can be self-inflicted or forced on us by others. Either way, the effects can be very damming and long-lasting.

Shame is created a variety of ways from many sources. Some you may already be familiar with, while others may have never crossed your mind. So where do shaming messages come from? Where do we place the blame? Do we blame generations of patterns that have been passed down? Do we blame the social determinants? Do we blame churches, faith organizations, or spiritual leaders for failing to provide a safe space to have open and honest conversations? Do we blame politicians, or do we blame institutions that create these systemic barriers? Is social media, internet, entertainment and the music industry to blame?

We live in a society that, in many ways, support shaming messages. Unfortunately, we are taught and even expected to perpetuate these messages. If you don't, then *shame on you*, you don't *fit in* with the status quo and then you are shamed even further for your individual stance. When we are filled with shame, we are more likely to shrink. We become withdrawn and isolated, which can lead to self-destructing behaviors that put us at risk mentally, emotionally, socially, financially, spiritually, and physically.

Morning Cup of F! That! with Coffee...
Thank You, Jesus, for reminding me how important individuality is! When I was in high school all those years ago, I along with a few others, was voted "most creative!" Out of the many things I have ever been called, I was truly honored to be called creative because that meant that I was an individual! It meant I marched to the beat of my own drum! It meant that I took risks! It meant that I was not afraid to be myself...all eclectic and bohemian. Over the years, I lost some of that individuality. Life happened! Fear happened! Insecurity happened! My individuality shrunk into a former shell of itself as I allowed myself to conform to societal norms, partner expectations, and a lot of other BS just to fit in. But Thank God He reminded me that I am uniquely, wonderfully, and fearfully made! I am an individual! I AM ME! In all the world, there is no one else exactly like me! F! fitting in, because first of all, that -ish doesn't feel right! And besides, it makes life boring and we miss out on so much while trying to fit in.

CHAPTER 3
I'M MELTING! WELL, SHRINKING....

What Happens When We Shrink?

"I'm getting smaller, Lou. Every day." ~The Incredible Shrinking Man (1957)

When I think about what shrinking looks like, I immediately visualize the scene from Wizard of Oz when the Wicked Witch is melting. In my mind, the depiction of the Wicker Witch melting is exactly what it feels like to shrink, your melting into a puddle of yourself and it's nothing you or anyone else can do to stop it from happening. I can tell you from first hand experiencing that shrinking does not feel good! Nor is it something I care to experience again.

So, what happens when we shrink? Shrinking will look different in everyone simply because we are all different. But in general, some things that may happen include:

- Low confidence
- Low self-esteem
- Depression
- Suicidal ideation
- Substance abuse
- Engaging in risky sexual behaviors
- Lack of trust in self and others
- Unhealthy and abusive relationship
- Lack of stability
- Unnecessary and unhealthy fear
- Anxiety
- Anger
- Internalized self-hatred
- Overcompensating

- Eating disorders
- Abnormal sleeping patterns
- Lack of care for appearance
- Isolation
- Giving up on life
- Lack of hope

If you have felt or experienced any of the aforementioned feelings, or engaged in any of the behaviors, it's time to fight for your life! It's time to fight to live! It's time to rewrite your story!

Grab your pen, because now the real work begins!

CHAPTER 4
F! THAT! RE-WRITE YOUR STORY

Morning Cup of F! That! with Coffee...
Thank You, Jesus! I didn't give up on me! I could have! I definitely felt like it! I could've ended it! It was definitely dark! It was very painful! It was the fight of and for my life! But...God! My Beloved! Don't you DARE give up on who you are!! F! That! and F! Those who don't get it or understand it! Fight like hell to be true to yourself, even if it means walking away from everything! Yup! Even those you love or that "love" you! Yes, it's hard, but it's not impossible!! Ask me how I know...I did it so I could live! I WANTED to LIVE! I HAD to LIVE so I could share my story with you!!

Give yourself permission!

As children, we lack the power and necessary skills to manage our lives. Our parents and other adults are pretty much in control over our lives. They tell us what to do, when to do it, and how to do it whether we like it or not. The great news is that now that we have become adults, we can change the trajectory of our lives because we are now in control of our lives, even if on some days we don't feel like it.

There will be times in our lives when we do not feel like we are in control and that's ok. However, it's not ok to throw yourself a pity party for the rest of your life. At some point, you have to put on your big girl panties or big boy drawers and face your -ish! As tough and painful as it may be, it is a necessary first step to creating the blueprint for the life you desire to live.

The single most difficult thing to do in life is to be ourselves! It would seem that being ourselves should be easy, right? NOT! It's actually quite challenging, especially with all the societal demands, partner requests, parental expectations, conditions, criteria, and pressure that we face. We get so wrapped up in all of this "stuff," that in the midst of it all, we disappear and become this person that everyone else wants us to be. We'd sacrifice ourselves rather than risk being authentic because that requires hard work.

And so we enter the comfort zone. We don't challenge conventional notions or buck the system because we don't like discomfort. We'd rather shrink than succumb to the scornful, judgmental eyes and thoughts of others. So we settle into this alternate version of ourselves...you know, the one that doesn't completely feel right, but as long as it's not too uncomfortable, we stay there. Well, here's the thing...not being who we are is waaaay more uncomfortable than being who we were created to be! And no matter what, we are still subjected to the random foolishness of others, regardless of who we choose to be--their version or ours. My Beloved, you gotta be YOU and I gotta be ME! We must fight unapologetically for the very thing that matters most in this world...the freedom to be ourselves! That's bold! That's courageous! That's real! All this other -ish about fitting in, toning down, scaling back, not being ourselves for the sake of other is BS! Don't get sucked into the illusion of life - this fantasy that we've been told for so long about who we must be. Man...F! That! I'm not a clone! I do not want to be anyone other than ME! I don't want to walk in anyone else's shoes! I have my own bad-ass pair of pumps that I rock out in! I AM ME! You can be YOU too! So what you gonna do? F! with it!

Let's get ready to rebuild your foundation!

Rebuilding Your Foundation

So, how do we rebuild from shrinking to living inspired and feeling empowered?

Moving from shrinking to living inspired and feeling empowered requires us to rebuild our foundation by pulling apart and dismantling all the damage caused by shrinkage. It requires courage, vulnerability and audacity because it focuses us to dig deep and face our imperfections, fears, doubts, unfounded beliefs, attitudes, and behaviors. You know all the -ish that we've been struggling with and/or running from. We must become unapologetic and intention in rebuilding our foundation. We must be willing to get a little bumps and bruises along the way.

When we dig deep, we develop authenticity. Authenticity is a daily practice of letting go of who others and we think we are supposed to be and embracing who we really are. Authenticity isn't always the *safe* **or** *popular* option, but it is the necessary option.

Rebuilding my foundation was not easy! In fact, I gave up a few times because I was met with a lot of opposition from many, including from those who should have been the ones supporting me along the way. The naysayers didn't believe that I was doing the right thing. They said I was selfish for doing things for myself. Some even went as far as to say I wouldn't make it. Nevertheless, I had to pick myself up, step out on faith, and trust and believe enough in myself to take the first step. Now of course, the first step is always the most difficult because you're unsure of what's waiting for you. You're unsure if you can do it. You're unsure if there will be challenges along the way, and you're unsure if you're going to be able to make it through those challenges. Yes, it's certainly a scary process because not only do you have to put yourself out there, which makes you extremely vulnerable, but now you also have to face your "stuff." And I don't' know how many of you have ever done this, but whew! It is very difficult because now you have to be honest with yourself and deal with all the -ish that you have been sweeping under the rug, stuffing in the closet, or covering up with designer labels. Who wants to do that? I know I sure didn't! While it was very difficult and sometimes even scary for me, it was also very necessary. It was something that I had to better myself. It was something I had to do if I wanted to be happy. It was something I had to do if I wanted to live; but most importantly, it was something that I had to do alone.

Having support is wonderful, and can be an extrinsic, outside motivating force; however, when deciding to make any change in your life, the motivation must be intrinsic or internal, meaning from within yourself. In other words, you must be your own cheerleader! You must be making the changes for yourself and only for yourself because if not, then you won't be as committed to the process and you're more likely to revert to old behaviors and/or give up. The more invested you are in your process, the greater result of growth you'll experience and the changes of you maintaining the changes increase significantly because it is something that you are doing because you have made a conscious decision to do.

A model that I used and continue to use to assist me with rebuilding my foundation is called the ***Empowered Consciousness Paradigm***. Together, these two words help to create a basis for a sturdy foundation because they are both building blocks in the process of growth.

To better understand the Empowered Consciousness paradigm, you must understand how each word works individually and together to maximize your experience and potential for growth.

Em pow ered [em-pou-er-ed]
TRANSITIVE VERB

Empowered refers to increasing the spiritual, emotional, social, intellectual, physical, and financial wellness of an individual and their environment. It often involves developing self-esteem and belief in one's own capacities. According to Wikipedia, empowerment is ultimately driven by the individual's belief in their capability to influence events in and around their lives.

The process of living an empowered life means listening to your inner voice, regardless of the pressure of family, friends, group belief systems, and society at large. It's trusting yourself enough to believe that you know what is best for you.

Living an empowered life allows you to gain the knowledge, skills, beliefs, and attitudes needed to effectively deal with the changing internal and/or external environments and circumstances.

Empowered living also includes the following:

- Having the power to make decisions regarding your life
- Having access to information and resources to help you make healthier and informed decisions
- Having the ability to be assertive
- Thinking positively regarding yourself and your situations
- Having high self-efficacy and belief in your abilities to make change
- Understanding the growth process and changes that are never ending and self-initiated
- Increasing positive self-image and overcoming stigma

In short, living empowered is the ability to function at the highest level of your consciousness to let go of self-defeating beliefs and behaviors and replace them with high self-esteem, self-efficacy, and loving affirmations and positive behaviors.

"Everyone has the capacity for greatness that transcends anything they have ever been taught to believe and knowing who you are confers that greatness and power to you."
~Wayne Dryer

Con·scious·ness [kon-shuh s-nis]
NOUN

- The state of being awake and aware of one's surroundings
- Awareness of something for what it is; internal knowledge
- Full activity of the mind and senses
- Awareness by the mind of itself and the world

Consciousness is innate self-awareness of one's personal identity, including the beliefs, attitudes, and behaviors. Consciousness also involves an awareness and understanding of how your beliefs, attitudes, and behaviors impact the world around you.

Cultivating self-awareness is a preliminary action in beginning to accept and embrace yourself. Self-awareness empowers you to seek growth, which gives you the power to change and become who you really desire to be. When self-awareness becomes your reality, you don't feel the need to fit into other's ideas of you, nor do you feel the need to justify who you are and what you believe.

Empowered and consciousness go hand and hand. They're like two peas in a pod, working together to give you your foundation for growth and change.

Empowered consciousness is grounded in the belief that once you have self-awareness or "consciousness" of how negative beliefs, attitudes, and behaviors are obstacles to empowerment that contribute to shrinking. Once you are aware of these obstacles/barriers, then you can effectively address and make the necessarily changes to prevent yourself from shrinking.

Grab Your Shovel and Start Digging!

The road to living inspire and feeling empowered is paved with gold. NOT! If it were so, we would never shrink! We would all be there rich with happiness and peace of mind. But since it's not, then we must be willing to do the work.

I don't think that change is something that we can ever be 100% ready for, even though it's always happening around us. Seasons change, times change, nothing stays the same. It's inevitable. It's is something that we all go through at some point in our lives and most of the time we're not in control of change. How we handle it is what determines how we grow.

Given the obstacles to living empowered and feeling inspired, some or all of which may affect any of us to varying degrees, how do we move toward empowerment? How do we remove the obstacles? How do we navigate the process? How do we re-write our story?

Empowering and sustainable change happens when we stay focused on our set of beliefs and we begin to align ourselves with the same kind of energy. We are what we attract not what we want. Additionally, for empowering and sustainable change to occur, there must be a process of *action* and *movement*.

It begins with a shift in your consciousness thought patterns by removing negative and cyclic patterns of shrinking behaviors and replacing them with an "F! That! I refuse to shrink!" attitude. You might be thinking that this sounds too good to be true. However, I challenge you to wrap your mind around the Empowered Consciousness way of life: *faith* (belief) + *action* (perseverance) + *movement* (patience) = *a life of living inspired and feeling empowered.*

- **Faith** is your belief in your ability. It's a system by which you live and believe.
- **Action** is something that we can do. It's steps that we take. It requires perseverance. Without perseverance, there is no action.
- **Movement** is a process that happens over time. The word process here implies growth as a result of continuous ongoing practice.

Faith is the seed. Action start the process of change, but without ongoing practice/perseverance, action cannot create enough momentum for real movement--that only happens over time with patience.

By committing yourself to following the Empowered Consciousness Paradigm (way of life) you are one step closer to saying, "F! That!" and living the life you so desire! The Empowered Consciousness Paradigm will help you incorporate small, steps into your daily life so you are less likely to revert to old shrinking behaviors and patterns. No matter what your previous unhealthy behaviors, the guidance and steps offered within the Empowered Consciousness Paradigm can help motivate you to improve your overall state of wellness.

Part of making lifestyle changes requires adopting new behaviors and changing how you live. Sometimes, we forget that changing everything at once can be overwhelming and we end up reverting back to old behaviors. Change can be difficult or easy depending upon how you view the process. Recognize that there may be a transitional period between the old and new behaviors and you may vacillate between your former behavior and thinking patterns, but don't be discouraged. This is normal when making any behavior change. I encourage you to set benchmarks for progress, acknowledge every effort you make, and be gentle and loving to yourself along the way.

Ownership is the key to saying, "F! That!" Truly, you have to dig deep inside your soul to own it. You must be willing to go against the status quo and become comfortable walking in your own pair of sexy heels, boots, gym shoes, flip-flops, or ballerina flats!

The key to ownership is learning to accept and love yourself in all your colors, and yes even the part that you so desire to change because you're confident in knowing that change will occur over time. Learning to trust and follow the divine spirit within yourself will enable you to find the strength and courage to own all that is authentically yours. And as you begin to embrace the divine spirit within you, you will possess the capacity to manifest and attract all your desires, wants, needs and/or beliefs; and that my Beloved is true empowerment!

As you begin to live your truth, it becomes easier to develop your empowered consciousness. It's easier to say, "F! That! I refuse to shrink!"

"When the pupil is ready, the teacher will appear." ~Unknown

Morning Cup of F! That! with Coffee...
Thank You, Jesus, for the call to action! Action can be defined as the process of getting something done. It's moving--with purpose--to accomplish something we desire! It's stepping out on faith, believing the impossible, and seeing the invisible. Often, we complain and gripe about things, but we fail to move in faith to take action. We do not actually take the steps to creating or providing solutions to the challenges that we complain about. So, what's the point of complaining? It's one thing to sit back and talk about what *needs* to or *should* be done. But it's another thing to get up off our butt and out of our comfort zone and move into action. If we don't take action, we don't see results! We don't see change! Action is just like faith--without works, it's dead! So, what does action look like? Action is offering a creative solution to a problem, creating a plan to accomplish it, and then enthusiastically accomplishing each step. It's getting out here in these streets and making some noise. It's standing up and fighting for what you believe in regardless of what society, family, or friends say; even if you have to stand alone! It's offering a helping hand to those who are out there actually doing the work. It's modeling the change or action that you want to see. Here's what action is NOT: Action is not expecting others to do it and complaining when they don't or if they don't

do it your way. It's not sitting at your computer, posting status updates about how things need to change. It's not blocking or hating on the efforts of others that are out here doing the work. It's not sitting around "the table," talking cute and coming up with great ideas that never materialize. My Beloved, we need to be about that action! What do you need to take action on right now? What are you going to do about it? I'm calling you out! I'm calling you to action! For everything you've ever complained about or wanted to change, here's your opportunity! Take at least one action step towards addressing it TODAY! Just one! That's a beautiful start! F! waiting on someone else to take action! Kick fear to the side and step over comfort! It's time to move something!

CHAPTER 5
SHRINK NO MORE!

Now that we have laid our foundation with the Empowered Consciousness Paradigm, we can begin rebuilding the rest of our structure.

It's time to transform judgment into love, do away with labels, dispel myths and start replacing them with messages of empowerment. So how do we begin to F! That? It's time to take back our power and reclaim the number one spot in our lives. Loving ourselves first must become the priority!

How do we do this?

Many of us have been on a flight before. Prior to take off, the flight attendant reviews safety procedures in case there is a loss of cabin pressure, they instruct the passengers to "Secure your mask tightly first before assisting others." My Beloved--that is exactly what we need to do! We are losing cabin pressure and we're shrinking! In order to save our lives, we need to secure our mask tightly!

Morning Cup of F! That! with Coffee...
Many people have asked me what this whole "Morning Cup of F! That! with Coffee" thing is all about. My answer is very simple: It's about me! That's not selfish either: it's self-preservation! It's a celebration of self-love! It comes from a place of genuine authenticity, vulnerability, and transparency! Man...I have been through soooo many things in my life that I have allowed them to hold me back. I have allowed soooo many people, especially those close to me, to stand in the way and prevent me from doing things that I really loved, or wanted to do, all because of their fear, disagreement, lack of understanding, or discomfort. In doing all of this, I lost me. I was depressed! I was unhappy! I was broken! I was fighting! Fighting for the right to be! Fighting for the right to breathe! Fighting for the right to feel my heartbeat! Fighting for the right to live MY LIFE! In the

process, I died! Now that I am on the other side of things, I have learned that being who I am regardless of what others think, feel, do, believe, or decide is essential! It's the only way to live! I cannot be there for anyone if I can't present and show up as ME! That's all I got, y'all! If you can't feel me or understand me, then F! That! That's your -ish to deal with! My worth, my life is too beautiful to be suffocated to death! So, when I say F! That, I MEAN That! No disrespect intended. I'm just unapologetically ME! My Beloved, everyone will always have something to say, from now until forever! You gotta be bold enough, fearless enough, and crazy enough to say...F! THAT! It's not rude or disrespectful, it's just being authentic and unapologetically honoring YOU! They, them, and the others will catch on later. If not, then F! That! Don't die for they, them, and the others! LIVE for you!!! YES, LIVE FOR YOU!!! Any questions?

My Beloved, now it's your turn to learn the not so subtle art of "F! That!"

CHAPTER 6
THE NOT SO SUBTLE "F! THAT!"

Enough is enough!

During my first marriage and prior to going through my divorce, I became numb and forlorn. I was lost in the thickets and trying to find my way out. I was in the abyss of hopelessness and despair. I had shrunk, and I was in distress. I was in dire need of an SOS!

SOS

Down in flames
crash and burn
ashes to be scattered among the Earth
my heart trampled like dried roses in memory of
I mourn
tears trickle into a puddle of me and my fantasies
of what we used to be
now betrayed by a wandering eye
accompanied by a lustful heart
and just to think why would result in the death of the rest of me
for misery has become my friend by day and a true lover by night
as I fight to stay afloat
sinking
I am sinking
sending out an SOS
will I be saved this time
or left to drift into the abyss far and beyond
I wonder
if the remnants of this scattered and shattered broken heart can be made whole
again

and by what ...love
will it answer my call....
©2006 TaMara Dillard (Dr. TaMara Griffin)

During this time, I wondered, 'Why me? When is enough, enough?" My mother would always tell me "TaMara, only you will know when enough is enough. Only you can make that determination." This uncertain state of being continued for about two years. But I'll be doggone if I did not wake up one morning, sit straight up in the bed, and decide that enough was enough! If I did not take back my power and control of my life, I was going to continue to shrink until I spiraled downward into a depression that I may not have been able to overcome. I made up my mind that muggy September morning that I was going to do something about that.

What did I do?

First, I decided that I wanted to live. Second, I decided that I was tired of shrinking, so I stepped out on **faith**. Third, I took **action**! I looked at myself in the mirror and I reluctantly began to face my -ish! Fourth, I began to dig deep. Fifth, I established a new foundation. Sixth, I began to re-write my story. Finally, which didn't come until many years later, I learned the subtle art of, "F! That!"

Interestingly enough, as I reached the seventh step and began learning the subtle art of "F! That!" I realized that the "F" represented much more than I could possibly imagine. The Fs were all action verbs:

1. Forgive
2. Face
3. Forget
4. Fancy
5. Feel
6. Find
7. F*ck (Ok, get your mind out of the gutter! It's not what you think. Then again, maybe it is! Keep reading and find out!)

On a subconscious level, these seven Fs had been the catalyst to propelling me into a negative cyclical pattern of shrinking behaviors. Since the seven Fs had crept into my consciousness, I could examine the role that each of the Fs played in helping me shrink and the role that each would play in the **movement** towards living inspired and feeling empowered.

Forgive That!

"When the wound is deep, the pain is haunting, and the scar feels like it will never heal, how do I forgive? The answer...start with yourself!" ~Dr. TaMara

We must forgive **all** the people, things, situations, and circumstances who hurt us, including ourselves. Maya Angelou said that forgiveness is one of the greatest gifts you can give yourself. Mahatma Gandhi believed that forgiveness was a characteristic of the strong. Sounds crazy, right? Years ago, I would have definitely agreed, but having been in this space a time or two myself, I can truly agree that forgiveness is powerful!

I know, I know...forgiveness is not easy, but I will tell you that it's necessary. How do you forgive someone who has hurt you, especially those who hurt you intentionally? How do you just turn the other cheek and walk away? How do you not?

One of the reasons we find it challenging to forgive is because we think that it means that we're OK with what happened. Forgiveness also seems hard because we attach it to weakness. We symbolize it with 'letting go' and that means setting the other person free. Well, here's the good news: forgiveness doesn't mean what happened was OK, nor does it mean that the person who hurt you should still be welcome in your life.

Another reason why we deliberately do not forgive is that we want to dwell on to the things that hurt us so that we can repeatedly blame the other person. Sometimes we tend to move away from taking responsibility for our mistakes. Forgiveness is not something we do for others--it's something we do for ourselves. In fact, no one benefits more from forgiveness than we do. When we refuse to forgive, we force ourselves to keep living in our painful memories and the scars never heal. We begin to carry the heavy emotions of anger, hate, resentment, and sadness over circumstances that we cannot change. These emotions eventually take root in our spirit and ultimately destroys us.

Forgiveness is about freeing ourselves of that burden. Forgiveness simply means that we have made peace with the pain; we're ready to let it go and move on with our lives. It's about taking back our power and becoming the hero rather than the victim in our lives.

Of course, I never said forgiveness was easy. It is definitely a challenging process. It can take months, sometimes years to forgive someone; nevertheless, forgiveness is an essential part of healing.

It's an important part of re-writing your story. When we choose forgiveness, we are not saying that what happened to us was okay. We're just making the choice not to allow ourselves to be held captive any longer. We're allowing ourselves to break free from the parts of our past that still hurt us in the present.

"Sincere forgiveness isn't colored with expectations that the other person apologizes or change. Don't worry whether or not they finally understand you. Love them and release them. Life feeds back truth to people in its own way and time." ~ Sara Paddison, author of The Hidden Power of the Heart

The first step in forgiveness is making a conscious decision to let go of resentment, bitterness, and any thoughts of revenge by identifying what needs healing and who needs to be forgiven and for what. The second step is to acknowledge honestly the role and/or choices you made in the situation. Third, try to reach a place of understanding and compassion without attaching any expectations to the process may be helpful in the journey to forgiveness. Fourth, make peace with the fact that the person or persons that hurt you, may never apologize or change. Getting another person to change his or her actions, behavior, or words isn't the point of forgiveness. Think of forgiveness more about how it can change your life. Fifth, release them to love and move forward with your life. No matter what steps you take during your process, choosing to forgive yourself and others will be worthwhile.

Although I had forgiven my ex-husband and many other people who I felt had done me wrong, in some way or another, I had not forgiven *myself*! I had hurt myself more than anyone could ever hurt me! I had allowed those things to happen to me because I chose to ignore my intuition. I chose to settle for anything, instead waiting for something that I truly deserved. Now, of course, that's not to say that other people intentionally or unintentionally made choices to hurt me, use me, and abuse me, because they certainly did! However, I also had to *acknowledge* and *forgive* the choices that I made that would ultimately result in my shrinking. I had to make peace with the fact that he and the others may never apologize or change. Once I begin to put the steps into practice, my life brightened. I was able to release my ex-husband to love. Again, that's not to say that what he did to me wasn't extremely hurtful, BUT I had finally made an honest and actively choice not to allow that pain to have a starring or recurring role in my life! It's too heavy and too taxing! I'm so happy that I can honestly say that I wish him nothing but the best!

My Beloved, it's time for you to forgive those who hurt you so that you can be free to move forward with your life!

"You will know that forgiveness has begun when you recall those who hurt you and feel the power to wish them well." ~Lewis B. Smedes, author of Forgive and Forget

<u>*Morning Cup of F! That! with Coffee...*</u>
I am so grateful for forgiveness! Sometimes forgiveness is a bitter pill to swallow, but it is so necessary that we do to heal our spirits! When we don't forgive someone or ourselves, it has power over us and we cannot move forward into all that God has planned for us. We also say, "I can forgive but not forget." Forgetting still harbors resentment and animosity, and that possesses power over us that prevents us from experiencing life to the fullest! Let us not spend so much time stressing, worrying, and thinking about what we or others have done to us; especially when oftentimes people don't even know that they've wronged us. Instead, let us move forward with a forgiving spirit and a heart of love. We'll never know when we'll need to be forgiven one day. I know there's been plenty of times I've needed it and thank God He has and others have too!

<u>Face That!</u>

What are you afraid to face?

I must admit that sometimes, I don't like looking in the mirror because that means I have to face my -ish! I have to face all my imperfections. I have to face all the things that I do not like about myself, and I have to face the brutal reality that some things about my physical appearance have changed. I am not as young as I used to be. My skin is not as clear as I would like. My body is not as toned as it used to be. I just have to face the fact that I am not "the average 20-year old girl sitting around counting the days...I'm now the old chick in the club." Ouch, that hurts! But as much as it hurts and as tough as it may be, I have to be honest and face my -ish! I have to learn to deal with it in a way that's helpful and not hurtful! And if I want things to change, I have to put in the work to fix it! Or instead of facing my -ish, I can pretend it doesn't exist, and live in a fantasy world until one day, it all comes to a head and I combust into a million pieces of myself.

I think I'd rather face my -ish!

Facing our -ish is one of the hardest things to do! Trust me, I know! I have been there a time or two, more than I care to admit. However, each time I did the work I became a much better version of myself like TaMara 2.0, 3.0, 4.0, 5.0...you get the picture.

49

On some level, we are all afraid of facing ourselves. We are afraid of what we might see. So instead of facing ourselves, we hide behind a mask. We avoid! We pretend! The problem with this is that when we hide behind a mask instead of facing our -ish, we block ourselves from experiencing the best life possible. However, when we dig deep and face our -ish, we find our truth! We find our light. We begin to find safety in becoming our authentic self.

My Beloved it's time to take off the mask, dig deep and face your -ish!

Morning Cup of F! That! with Coffee...
I am so grateful that I've learned how to dig deep and face my -ish! We all have to work through many layers of ourselves to get to the root cause of our stuff. However, instead of digging deep, most of us just stop at the superficial/ outer layer. You know the one where we try to make others and ourselves believe that we have it all together. Occasionally, we go to the inner layer where we may acknowledge something to ourselves but do nothing about it. Rarely, if ever, do we go to the root layer- cause of our -ish because it requires us to dig deep. When we dig that deep, we have to face our -ish? That's tough! But if we really want to make significant changes or grow, then we have to put in the work and dip deep! There's no easy way around it. My Beloved, it's time to get knee deep in it! It's time to start digging deep! Grab your shovel, put your boots on, and start digging up your -ish! It may take some time, but it will be well worth it! My favorite dessert of all time is a chocolate molten lava cake! Yummmmmmy! A chocolate molten lava cake is a dome-shaped chocolate cake that is topped with confectioners' sugar and filled with hot melted chocolate on the inside. When you look at the cake, it looks beautiful! It's well put together! It's served with strawberries, ice cream, chocolate drizzle, small chocolate beads and mint leaves. However, it's not until you scrap the surface, break through the outer layer and dig deeper that the "good stuff," the melted chocolate comes oozing out! You see the melted chocolate doesn't come out right away and it won't unless you dig deep! F! the confectioners' sugar and the cake! I don't want just the surface sugar and outer layer of cake! I want the good stuff! I want the molten lava! In order to get to it, I have to put in the work and dig deep! When I do, it's sooooo worth it and it taste so damn good!

Hold on now before we get all excited and ready to run off and start digging, I must warn you that facing that (our -ish) also involves facing our fears, worries and doubts. That's going to be scary because fear can shatter our sense of the world as we know it!

"The only thing we have to fear is fear itself." ~Franklin D. Roosevelt

It has been said that life is ninety percent of what we worry about or fear will happen. The other ten percent is what actually happens. We spend so much time fearing fear. Too often, we allow fear, worry, doubt, obstacles, challenges, barriers, etc. to dominate and define our lives. We allow them to keep us from moving forward. They steal our joy and kills our dreams. We hold back and play it safe, to avoid rejection, feeling embarrassed, looking silly, being hurt, possible failure or even success. We hold back because we fear that we will shrink.

"The only way to deal with fear is to face it. This means we must stretch ourselves beyond our comfort zone." ~Dr. TaMara

At some point in our lives, we all must face our fears, worries, doubts, or some obstacle, challenge or barrier that seems insurmountable. The question is, how will we respond? Our response has the power to change the trajectory of our lives. We have to be willing to take a leap of faith despite being afraid, worried, or doubtful. Situations take us beyond our comfort zone and trigger our uncomfortable emotions have the power to become moments of authenticity.

Don't be afraid to feel the fear!

In order to find our authentic self and live inspired and feel empowered we must face our fears, confront our worries, and address our doubts by digging down to the deepest, most hidden part of ourselves; that part of ourselves that we run from. Learning to lean in to discomfort and experience your emotions, difficulties, challenges, etc. without resistance, will empower you to face that, your -ish.

My Beloved, the time has come for you to face your stuff and confront your fears. You're at a crossroads in your life. It's time for you to move forward and stop allowing yourself to shrink out of fear, worry, and doubt. It's time to overcome challenges, barriers, and obstacles.

How do I start? You must create a game plan!

- Ask yourself the following questions: What's actually going to happen? What's the worst? What's the best?
- Go inward to evaluate your fears, worries, doubts and put them into perspective
- Identify ways to address potential challenges, barriers or obstacles. Be

SMART about it – Specific, Meaningful, Attainable, Realistic and Timely. (See Appendix B)
- Create a plan to maintain a sense of personal control and accomplishment. Include short, medium and long-term goals
- Walk it out! Be present and actively engaged in the process. Even if it doesn't go completely as planned, don't give up!
- Extend yourself grace. Be loving and kind to yourself at all times.

Facing our stuff is unavoidable, and how we handle them reveals a deeper layer of who we are and what we care about most and that should be ourselves!

Like Nike says, *"just do it,"* even if you have to do it afraid!

Taking the first step is always the hardest... BUT YOU CAN DO IT!

Morning Cup of F! That! with Coffee...
I've learned to lean into the fear and face the discomfort! Comfort can be a dangerous thing! It can squeeze the life out of us! When we are too comfortable, we allow ourselves to settle for things, people and situations that aren't necessarily good for us. When we're comfortable, we're more likely to sit in the midst of the foolishness, no matter how crazy it is, because it's what we're used to. It's what we know. We'd rather operate in total chaos and functional dysfunction rather than move and risk being uncomfortable. I stayed in an abusive marriage because of comfort! Yes, it was abusive but I was comfortable in the midst of the mess. I knew what to expect from the ex! And when we know what to expect, that makes us comfortable. But check this out, comfort is also rooted in fear. So even though I knew what to expect, I was still afraid. I was afraid -not so much to leave my marriage, but more so afraid of what others would think of me leaving. So instead of risking the gossip and judgment of others, I stayed comfortable. I was also comfortable with the financial life he provided because, hell, after all he was making over six figures. At the time I was afraid that I could not support myself if I left. So, I settled for comfort. Because of comfort, I spent many days very unhappy! I wasted so many years of my life that I can not get back! Man...F! Comfort! I now live beyond the boundaries of comfort! I refuse to let the fear of being uncomfortable keep me settled for less than I deserve or want! My Beloved it's time to step out of the comfort zone! Putting ourselves in uncomfortable situations is essential to growth. What have you been wanting to do or say but you've allowed comfort to hold you back? Everything we want and need is right outside its boundaries. Now of course I don't expect us to go from 0 to 10 in one step however, we must

take steps even if that means going from 0 to 1. It's the movement that matters. And each time we step, it become a little easier to move. Don't let comfort stop you from becoming the best you! So...say it with me! And say it loudly!! "F! Comfort!" AGAIN! "F! Comfort!!!! I don't fear you! I fear living life never having done something that I really want to do!" Now that that's out of your way, GO DO IT!!

Forget That!

"Forget and forgive is that golden rule which helps us in taking away some wise lessons from our mistakes and yet moving forward without leaving any residues of anger and bitterness behind." ~Surabhi Surendra

Morning Cup of F! That! with Coffee...
Thank You, Jesus, that I've learned when to fold' em! It can be extremely difficult to make the decision to walk away from someone that we love, including family. As painful as it may be, sometimes it's the best thing we can do for ourselves and for them; because staying could result in certain disaster. In those trying times, we must come to understand that in order to move forward saying goodbye is the only option. We have to be open to the possibility that that particular person and/or relationship has served its purpose in our life. The season is over. Trying to hold on will only prolong the inevitable; making our grieving and healing process even longer. My Beloved, who and/or what are you holding on to unnecessarily? F! that! It's time to fold'em. Seasons must come to an end in order to continue evolution, growth and bring forth new life. So, as we move forth folding up the past, let us step out on faith and trust in God knowing that He does not close one door without opening another. So, chuck up the peace sign, holla, "deuces ...I'm good!" And keep it moving!

Disclaimer: Now before we go any further, it's imperative to remember that forgetting does not mean denying your true feelings about your experience or what happened. Denial will only lead to a bigger issue later on. However, forgetting does mean you acknowledge the experience and/or emotions attached to it and you've made an active choice to let it go.

We often attach ourselves to people, places, and things. We become so enraptured, that if or when we lose them, it can totally devastate us. We hold on so tight to every little thing that we literally end up squeezing the life out of it and us, and we shrink. Although we're in relationships, we love people, have nice things, and enjoy going places they are not our possessions. We don't own them! Trying to own and control people, places and things that don't belong to us only makes life miserable and ironically, in the end, we're the only ones being controlled. When we learn to detach ourselves and let go; it's actually then we begin to experience the beauty of life. We let go of the stress, worry, anxiety, depression, hurt, etc. associated with trying to control things that we really don't own in the first place. In order to truly have it all, in order to be free; we have to forget about the people, places, and things that no longer are beneficial to our growth.

Forgetting is a very close companion of forgiving. In fact, the two are besties. They go hand and hand and can help you learn to walk beautifully off into the sunset if you are willing to dig deep and stretch yourself.

One of the hardest things to do is to forgive *and* forget the source of your pain. It seems that if we forget, we are letting the source go free and we are approving of the action that caused us pain. But the truth is that forgetting, leads to peace. It does not set the other person free. It sets us free. It brings us peace of mind and makes our hearts lighter and releases us to be authentic with ourselves and others.

"Forgive but don't forget." We've all heard the phrase or even perhaps said the phrase ourselves. Simply forgiving does not help. When we don't forget, the moment that source or something similar to it flashes in our mind, we go deep in the thoughts of hurt and grudge. We must also forget, let go of that which is the source of our unhappiness. While forgiving helps in removing the incident or the source from the front of our mind, forgetting helps to release the anger, hurt pain and madness that continues to linger in the back of our minds. Our thoughts are bursts of energy. They affect us on a profound level. Forgetting helps us in getting rid of these emotional, mental, spiritual, energetical, and biochemical toxins that cause us to shrink.

"Not the power to remember, but very opposite, the power to forget, is a necessary condition for our existence." ~ Sholem Asch

My Beloved, just forget! Let bygones be bygones! You can't change or undo it, so just forget that! With time and with practice, we can eventually learn to let go, forgive and forget and sooner or later one day you'll find ourselves saying who did what? Oh yeah! I forgot about that because I decided to move on with my life!

"There are things that have to be forgotten if you want to go on living." ~ Stephen Carpenter

Morning Cup of F! That! with Coffee...
Today I'm so grateful that I've learned that it's not important to "get back" at others. When we're hurt, we want to get back at those that have hurt us. But in the end when we seek revenge we ultimately end up hurting

ourselves even more. And what's worse usually the person that we're trying to get back has gone on about their business; and were the ones left carrying the emotional scars and baggage. My Beloved, it's time to forget all of that "get back" anger that has been weighing our spirits down. Let it go and walk away. The best way we can get back at someone is to focus on ourselves and succeed at being the best we can be; it takes all the power away from them and gives it back to us! Forgive and forget! Allow our spirits to heal. "Love your enemies, do good to those who hate you, bless those who curse you, pray for those who mistreat you." We don't have to do anything to get revenge but just sit back and allow karma to unfold! For they shall reap what they sow. "Vengeance is mines, thus said the Lord."

Fancy That!

"Oh you fancy huh?
Oh you fancy huh?
Oh you fancy huh?
Oh you fancy huh?"

Canadian recording artist Drake so elegantly rapped about his woman being "fancy" in his number one US Billboard Hot Rap Song "Fancy" from his debut album Thank Me Later. Being fancy means owning our inner and outer beauty. When asked about his lyrics to Fancy, Drake stated, *"Women like to feel important. I don't want you to feel important because we all lust after you, but because you're individually beautiful."*

So, what does it mean to be *"fancy?"*

Noun, plural **fancies**.
1. Imagination or fantasy, especially as exercised in a capricious manner
2. The artistic ability of creating unreal or whimsical imagery, decorative detail, etc.

Adjective, **fancier, fanciest.**
1. Made, designed, grown, adapted, etc., to please the taste or fancy; of superfine quality or exceptional appeal

Verb (used with object), **fancied, fancying.**
1. To form a conception of; picture to oneself
2. To believe without being absolutely sure or certain

So, in essence being "fancy" means that we are Divine because we are made in His Image! We fit mind, body, spirit, and soul. We are tapping into and utilizing our creative unique and individual gifts and talents to transcend and transform. It also means to believe beyond a shadow of a doubt that we deserve to live the best life possible! Being fancy is not about living for the approval of or living for someone else! It's all about being fancy for your number one...you!

In order to be fancy, we must be authentic in our approach to living. This includes making sure we are fit in every **Dimension of Wellness** (emotional, mental, physical, spiritual, social, and financial, energetical). When we challenge ourselves within each dimension, we experience growth. However, when we fail to challenge ourselves in each dimension, we lack balance. As a result, we shrink and begin to suffer in each dimension. For example, when we are spiritually conflicted, we become emotionally and mentally stressed out. This stress begins to take a toll on us physically. We may become tired, fatigued, or sick. When we don't feel well, we tend to isolate ourselves and withdraw from social circles and settings. If we become too sick and too stressed out, we cannot go to work which begins to affect our finances. This chain of events begins to wreak havoc on our lives. If we don't find a way to address the initial concern and create balance, we shrink!

Actively being present in all the Dimensions of Wellness will help you begin to incorporate small steps into your daily life so you are less likely to engage in or revert back to old shrinking behaviors and patterns.

- Emotional Wellness - requires you to accept and manage your feelings, including your ability to understand your limitations, navigate through stressful situations, and develop and maintain healthy relationships with others.
- Mental Wellness - involves participating in creative, stimulating, growth-oriented activities that entail learning new skills and sharing that knowledge and those skills with others.
- Physical Wellness - helps you manage your physical health on a daily basis, monitor your diet, and increase your physical activity to a minimum of 30 minutes a day, five days a week.
- Spiritual Wellness - focuses on finding meaning and purpose in life and defining a value system to operate within. It also involves finding your balance and remaining centered in who you are.
- Social Wellness - focuses on friendships, social support networks, and comfortable interaction with others, and balance between personal and community environments.
- Financial Wellness - focuses on financial health by creating and

maintaining tools and strategies that will help to get and keep finances on track.

- Energetical Wellness – helps you learn how to be more careful with whom we allow in our spaces – physical, mental, and emotional. It also teaches the importance of protecting the sexual energy that we share with others.

Using the Dimensions of Wellness as your guide when developing your plan for improving your life will help to establish and maintain balance and it will also prevent you from shrinking.

Morning Cup of F! That! with Coffee…
I've learned to be more careful with whom I allow in my Dimensions. However, this was not always the case. Throughout the course of my life, I've definitely brought some unnecessary disappointment, heartache, grief, and loss to myself all because I wasted my energy and allowed some undeserving people and things into my space. At the time, I did not understand the importance of respecting and protecting my dimensions. I did not have the appropriate boundaries in place. Nor, did I have the courage to walk away or kick them out of my life. But thank God I've grown much wiser and stronger! I am now extremely careful with whom or what I share my energy and space. I am firm and unapologetic with my boundaries, even if it means letting some people and things go! I will not allow anyone or anything to deplete me! My Beloved, we must protect our dimensions: emotional, mental, physical, spiritual, social, and financial, energetical. It's so draining and uninspiring to be surrounded by venomous people who lack ambition, motivation, and/or passion for life. Their negativity is too much! It's overwhelming! Their energy is so strong that it can drag us right down into the depths of despair and hell; right along with them. Their space is so cluttered that it weighs us down and wears heavy on our spirit. The things that they bring into our life is detrimental to our very existence. After all, misery loves company and letting the wrong person or thing in can certainly result in a lifetime of misery! And besides, F! That! Everyone does not deserve the honor of receiving our energy or the privilege of being in our Dimensions, I don't care if it's spouses, partners, family members, friends, etc. It's time to clean house - figuratively and maybe even literally! Cleanse your space and energy TODAY! I got my sage burning as I write!

Being fancy also includes utilizing our gifts and talents. We have a responsibility to develop the gifts and talents we have been given. Sometimes we think we do not have many gifts or talents or that other people have been blessed with more abilities. We get so caught up in being focused on other's gifts and talents that we fail to utilize ours or we begin to compare ours to theirs.

Sometimes we do not use our gifts and talents because we are afraid that we might fail or be criticized by others. We should not hide our gifts and talents because when we do, we shrink because we are not being authentic! We are stifling a very critical part of who we are and/or want to be. We become miserable and unhappy.

My God! I shudder at the many times, even as an adult, I have allowed myself to shrink because others thought I was being too fancy! They and them thought that I was "doing too much," or that "it doesn't take all that," or "who does she think she is?" In those times, I killed my fancy all because I didn't want to bring attention to myself. I mean who wants to stand out like a sore thumb or who wants to be criticized by others for being "different," "weird," "dressing funny," etc. While it may be a little easier to overcome when it's someone who is not really close to you, it becomes particularly challenging when it's your spouse or partner, or friends and family members questioning your fancy. But thank God, I grew. What I realized was that they, them, and the others (even spouses, partners, family and friends) did not define me! I also had to realize that I deserved to have the best life possible, despite what they and them thought or felt! They and them could not determine how I lived my life. I had to determine who I wanted to be and how I wanted to live. I had to live my LIFE on my terms! Once I came to this realization, I became so fancy, like supa extra fancy! So, when I hear the phrase, "oh you fancy huh? I answer, "HELL YEAH, I'm fancy! Guess what My Beloved, you are fancy too! And it's time that we both start unapologetically owning it! F! That! It's time we start walking out our L.I.F.E.--Living Inspired and Feeling Empowered!

Be unpredictable! Be creative! Be Bold! Be Alluring! Be Sexy! Be Sensual! Be You! Be Fancy!

Morning Cup of F! That! with Coffee...Fancy That!
"They" and "them" ... family, friends, spouses, partners, parents, co-workers, siblings, etc... have us so F*cked up! Man... we're so concerned about what they say or how they feel, how to dress or how to share our gifts and talents. We're so afraid to take a chance, to make a mistake, to be embarrassed, to step out on our faith, to make a "fool" of ourselves all because of what they and them might think or might say. Because of this fear, we fail! We fail to live life! We fail to explore and experience God's best! We fail to walk boldly and courageously in our Purpose! We fail to pursue our passions! We fail at everything because we're so busy worrying about what they and them think or how they and them feel! As a result, we

shrink into this vision that others have for us and become settled into nothing. We don't push back, we don't test boundaries, we just simply settle into the safety of "others" comfort, judgment, and control. Here's the thing...that doesn't do anything for us! We don't grow by playing it safe according to their rules. We don't truly live without taking risk; regardless of how others feel or think. In order to truly be free, we have to be willing to be fancy! What power and freedom lies beyond the fear of being called a fancy! F! those who call you a fancy! They're too busy living in fear to experience freedom! They're too busy hiding behind the constantly changing blurred lines of "they," "them," and the societal constraints that try to keep us from being who we're really destined to be! My Beloved...you have a choice to make! You can continue living a life defined by others or we can become the fanciest of them all! Become the one that lives on purpose, takes chances, embraces and shares your gifts and talents, creates happiness, falls in love and loves hard, practices kindness, travels often, values people's, things and experiences, laughs every day, let's go, respects others, lives fearlessly, and goes confidently in the direction of our dreams and live the life you've always imagined! Now fancy that!

Find That!

I want to ask you a question. You don't have to answer it right now, but hopefully by the end of this section, you will have the answer.

What's keeping you from being happy? Whatever it is, it's time to find that!

Morning Cup of F! That! with Coffee...
Thank You, Jesus, for helping me find happy! For a time in my life, I struggled with being happy. As I reflect on that time in my life, I realize that I wasn't happy because I wasn't being true to who I was. I was too busy trying to please everyone else. I was too busy trying to be everything to everyone else that my life became a mess! It was complicated and unbalanced. Boundaries were blurred. I was very unhappy to the point of losing myself because I allowed too many people to define, drain, deplete, and depend on me. Don't get me wrong there's nothing wrong with supporting and being there for others; however, the key is balance, perspective, boundaries, and priorities. Once I began to put things into proper perspective, I created boundaries, began prioritizing, all of which created balance. I found myself! I found happiness! And F! ever letting happy go again! My Beloved, what's standing between you and happy? Let's take a long intense look into our spirit. Let's search the depths of our soul. Let's stop allowing other people to drain, deplete, and continuously take from us. Let's stop looking to other people, places or things to be our happy when we already have the power to do so ourselves. We have to be

willing to become our #1 priority, change our perspective, and create boundaries. That's not selfish! That's self-preservation! Once we do this, we shall dance a beautifully balanced dance with happy! So...like rapper, singer, songwriter and record producer Pharrell sang: "clap along if you feel like happiness is the truth (Because I'm happy) clap along if you know what happiness is to you (Because I'm happy)!

"I believe that the very purpose of life is to be happy. From the very core of our being, we desire contentment. In my own limited experience I have found that the more we care for the happiness of others, the greater is our own sense of well-being. Cultivating a close, warmhearted feeling for others automatically puts the mind at ease. It helps remove whatever fears or insecurities we may have and gives us the strength to cope with any obstacles we encounter. It is the principal source of success in life. Since we are not solely material creatures, it is a mistake to place all our hopes for happiness on external development alone. The key is to develop inner peace." ~Dalai Lama

The one thing in life besides love that most of us all want is to be happy! What's interesting about this is that we all wish to achieve that magical state of happiness that has never truly been defined, yet everyone seems to chase after it. Some people equate happiness to material things, money, success, love, possessions, etc. however when we try to measure happiness against those tangible ideals, it doesn't quite line up. Material things lose value, money comes and goes, success is fleeting and love, well that's a whole another topic and we really don't possess anything especially not people.

So, you might be asking since happiness cannot be measured with tangible things, then how do we measure happiness? What does happiness really look like? The answer...happiness just is! Happiness is a state of being! Happiness, like other emotions, is not something you find but rather something you embody. It's just something we either are or aren't. When we understand this truth, then we can discover happiness in just about anything.

Since happiness is all about being, then how do we become happy. I'm so glad you ask. We become happy by becoming our ideal self, by ourselves and for ourselves. I hate to be the bearer of bad new but umm, we have this whole being happy thingy f'ed up! We've been sold this fairytale that others are responsible for making us happy. Don't believe the hype! It's the biggest crock of BS! Our happiness is our responsibility! When we shift that responsibility to others, not only do we usually end up disappointed, but it diminishes our power over our lives and it doesn't force us to be accountable to facing our -ish! Additionally, when we stop placing the responsibility on others for our happiness, we're less likely to shrink because we have allowed them to disappoint us. We must stop looking for happiness outside of ourselves and start realizing that WE are our own happiness! Learn to lean into the ideal that when we are living our authentic lives, regardless of what society, family, spouses, partner, or friends says we experience inner peace and we give ourselves permission to be happy.

So again, I ask you, "What's stopping you from being happy?" The answer is YOU! Now that you know, what are you going to do about it?

Morning Cup of F! That! with Coffee...

Man...F! that! Life is waaaay too short to be unhappy! We're here today and gone tomorrow yet we spend this brief amount of time under the scrutiny of others! We spend this time allowing others to dictate our path! We spend this time in unfulfilling relationships that ultimately contribute to our demise! And for what???! Because we're afraid of what "them" and "they" will have to say about OUR life? Are you kidding me???! We allow outside influences to have waaaay too much say and/or control in how we navigate OUR lives! We allow individuals, situations, and experiences to determine OUR destiny instead of living life on OUR terms and standing firm in OUR truths and convictions. Now, don't get me wrong, I am certainly NOT saying that we should be obnoxious, rude, hateful, disrespectful, or inconsiderate of others. However, I AM saying that we have to live OUR lives according to what makes us happy! Happiness is a combination of positive emotions, intention, energy, flow, and esoteric meaning ascribed to our experiences. Happiness is staying grounded, connected, and consciously aware. Happiness is being present in the moment and our five senses. Happiness is nurturing our spirit and feeding our soul! Happiness is that Divine connection to other's inner being! Happiness is a state of being not a onetime experience or pursuit. When we lack any of the aforementioned, we are not happy, and we suffer in one or all dimensions of our life! My Beloved, are you truly happy? If not, it's time to be! It's not selfish to want to be happy! Society, friends, family and partners would have us to believe this -ish! They feed us this belief for a couple of reasons: 1) it's a way of controlling us, 2) they fear of our shine, 3) the lack of understanding regarding our desire for happiness and/or 4) they don't know how to be happy themselves, so they block our attempt. Misery loves company and fears what it does not understand! The unfortunate thing about this is that when society, family, friends, and/or partners hold on too tight or back us in to a corner, we begin to resent them, and they usually end up losing us anyway. It's just best to allow someone to be their happy! So today, in spite of what everyone thinks or says...it's time to get yo' happy...whatever that is for you! You don't have to make a big or drastic move...just make one! Do something for YOU that's going to allow you to be happy, put a smile on your face, and bring peace to your heart!

Feel That!

"I am the master of my emotions –
I transform fear to love, anger to compassion,
pain to comfort, scarcity to abundance,
expectation to gratitude, and jealousy to generosity."
~Jonathan Lockwood Huie

I am a super emotional person. I feel everything! I cry at the drop of a dime. I have been known to cry because the wind blows the wrong way. For most the part, I am able to express my emotions in a healthier way, but there are times when my emotions become overwhelming and really challenging to manage. When this happens, I dig deep to figure out how to effectively navigate and express what I am feeling. You know, what's interesting is that when I was younger, I hide my emotions. I never showed any emotions, especially not in front of others partly because I was shy and because I did not want to be judged. I would hold in whatever I was feeling until I was alone. My mantra was "never let 'em see you sweat." I felt like if anyone saw me sweat or show emotions, that they would take advantage/ make fun of my vulnerability and, oh no!--I couldn't have that. I got older, I began to realize how unhealthy it was for me to hide emotions, so I began writing in a journal. This became a very therapeutic way to express what I was feeling without judging. When we judge our emotions, we strip them of their ability to teach us. I realized that I was the master of my emotions, whatever they are! I realized that expressing my emotions was a very human thing to do. It purges the negative and cleanses the spirit and soul. Positive emotions help us to elevate our mood and enjoy life. I learned that our emotions are our teachers. When we are open to feeling and exploring our emotions, we can learn a lot about ourselves. Everyone feels emotions regardless of your gender, sexual orientation, biological sex, age, ability, socioeconomic status, race, or ethnicity. I am so grateful for my emotions! They are an intricate part of me! The help to experience the vitality of life in a powerful and unforgettable way!

"Emotions are the heart of humanity." ~Dr. TaMara

As children, many of us, especially men, were taught that emotions are to be hidden, especially if those emotions weren't considered "natural" for your gender. (eyeroll) Although men are no more immune from emotions than women, women are considered to be "emotional" because society has taught us that it is OK for women to express certain emotions and cry; however, women are not to express anger or dissatisfaction because then she's considered a bitch. Men, of course, are taught to suck it up when they are hurt. They are also taught not to show love or be vulnerable because it's considered a sign of weakness. The very unfortunate part of this is that we eventually became adults that do not know how to effectively express or handle our emotions. This contributes to many challenges that we face, such as relationship issues and expressing our emotions in a negative or unhealthy way.

Emotions can play an important role in how we think and behave. Emotions can be fleeting, persistent, powerful, complex, and life changing. They can motivate us to act and influence the decisions that we make.

Part of having a full and meaningful life is experiencing the complete range of your emotions, both pleasant and unpleasant. We cherish and look forward to pleasant emotions like happiness, love, and joy. However, because life happens we will not always be able to experience the pleasant emotions. We will sometimes have to deal with unpleasant, shrinking emotions. We are often taught that we should try to avoid unpleasant emotions at all costs. When we bottle up our emotions, they sit in our body, and we become affected. We to try to escape from those feelings through alcohol, drugs, restricting food, binging, busy-ness, compulsive sex, or other self-harming behaviors that cause us to shrink. Hurt, frustration, pain, sadness, and anger are all natural and healthy parts of the human experience.

Our emotions are often messengers that signal something important that we need to pay attention to. Every feeling, good or bad, happy or sad, has a message. Emotions demand to be felt. Rather than trying to suppress your feelings, work to be a mindful observer of them. Notice the emotions that you experience and where you feel them in your body. If you don't consciously allow the feeling, they will find a way to make themselves known. We must learn to "lean into" our emotions and experiences them authentically. Then, try to cultivate a curious and nonjudgmental stance. Processing our feelings helps us tap into our own inner wisdom and creativity. When we begin to truly embody and experience all our emotions, we begin to shift and transform our lives.

There are many healthy ways to process your emotions. Below are some helpful tools that I used to really embody and experience my emotions:

• Journaling my feelings
• Creating artwork that represents my feeling
• Meditating
• Acknowledging and confronting my honest emotions
• Seeking insight from a therapist

Morning Cup of F! That! with Coffee...

I'm so thankful for emotions! Emotions are the heart of humanity. Emotions connect us with one another. Emotions help us to experience life in all its colors! Man... I am a super emotional person. I can't hide it very well. You can see it in my eyes! I cry when the wind blows the wrong way. I can't see hurt and not feel some sort of way. I feel everything! And although emotions can be very draining, they can be very life giving. When I was younger though, I remember not showing emotions or "never letting them see me sweat" because I thought that if "they"--whoever the heck "they" are--saw me show my emotions they would think that I was weak or that they got the best of me. So instead of crying, getting angry or showing some emotion, I kept it in. And what good did that do besides manifest itself in some other way within me? The unfortunate thing about emotions is that we are taught that we're not supposed to have any, or if we do, we're not supposed to show them. Boys/men better not cry, right? If they do cry or show some emotion, they're weak or "acting like a little girl." Girls/ women can show emotion but if we show too much, then we're being too "extra" or a "drama queen." Or better yet, both are acting like a b*tch! What kind of foolish -ish is that? What the heck is "too emotional?" That's like saying too human! God gave us emotions to express when spoken words cannot effectively convey or capture the true essence of what we're feeling. God gave us emotions to connect with humanity, to feel what others and we are going through so that we could practice compassion. God gave us emotions to help cleanse our spirits and heal! My Beloved, life is all about emotions! It's all about feeling and using our five senses to experience and express it! That's why people snap, because they didn't express their emotions and they became so overwhelmed that they couldn't deal with it anymore. And that's one reason why our partners leave because they didn't feel emotionally connected to us. How the heck could we live every day without experiencing any feeling toward anyone or anything? That's not living that's existing in some sort of non-human like state. F! That! I want to feel my emotions! It helps me to feel alive! And I'll take living any day! Who wants to walk around looking like a stone face every day, all hard and -ish! Isn't that uncomfortable? Try expressing your emotions to someone today! I love y'all. Now, see how easy that was? And it felt so darn good!

F*ck That!

"There is nothing more rare, nor more beautiful, than a woman being unapologetically herself; comfortable in her perfect imperfection. To me, that is the true essence of beauty."
~Steve Maraboli, behavioral scientist and author

We all have an inner voice. Sometimes it decides to make its presence known and right now mines is yelling F*ck That! F*ck That! F*****CK THAAAAAT!!!! Sorry, not sorry! We have to become unapologetic about L.I.F.E. - living inspired and feel empowered! We can no longer allow anyone or anything to stand our way! It's a choice, our choice! IT'S OUR CHOICE!

My Declaration of Self-Esteem "I AM ME"

In all the world, there is no one else exactly
like me. Everything that comes out of me is authentically me.
Because I alone chose it. I own everything about me
My body, my feelings, my mouth, my voice, all my actions.
Whether they be to others or to myself . I own my fantasies,
My dreams, my hopes, my fears. I own all my triumphs and
successes, all my failures and mistakes.
Because I own all of Me, I can become intimately acquainted with me. By so doing
I can love me and be friendly with me in all my parts. I know
there are aspects about myself that puzzle me, and other
aspects that I do not know. But as long as I am
Friendly and loving to myself, I can courageously
and hopefully look for solutions to the puzzles and for ways to find out more about me
I look and sound, whatever I say and do, and whatever
I think and feel at a given moment in time is authentically
Me – If later some parts of how I looked, sounded, thought
and felt turn out to be unfitting, I can discard that which is
keep the rest, and invent something new for that
which I discarded
I can see, hear, feel, think, say, and do
I have the tools to survive, to be close to others, to be
productive to make sense and order out of the world of
people and things outside of me
I own me, and therefore I can engineer me – I am me and I am ok.

© *Virginia Satir, 1975.*

This is one of my favorite poems! In fact, I use this poem quite frequently with the many women and girls that I work with.. I was introduced to this poem by my high school communications teacher, Ms. Barrett. From the moment I read it, I fell in love! It spoke to me in ways I couldn't imagine. It somehow gave me the strength to be myself.

My Declaration of Self- Esteem, "I AM ME," was originally written in 1975 by Virginia Satir. She originally wrote this poem for a teenage girl who sent her a question asking her, "How can I prepare myself for a fulfilling life?"

I never realized until I was researching for this book, that this poem was written for a teenage girl nor that it was written in 1975, the year I was born. Now, I understand the Divinity of this poem. I understand why I gravitated towards this poem. I understand why it has resonated in my Spirit over the years. This poem was written for me! I was a teenage girl the first time I read this poem. And I am reminded each and every time that I read this poem that I AM ME!

This is among one of the greatest and timeless self-esteem affirmations written. When asked about the poem, Virgina stated: "we must not allow other people's limited perceptions to define us." This means that you and I must learn to say, "F*ck That!" We must learn to accept all of ourselves and be of all ourselves, in all our colors, with all our imperfections, unapologetically!

Many people--myself included--live lives full of apologies. We apologize for being who we are, how we feel, what we think, and what we do. We apologize for being ourselves. This is one of the most harmful things we can do to ourselves because it causes us to shrink each and every time we apologize. Throughout my life, I have shifted back and forth between shrinking and being my unapologetic self. During those moments when I weren't true to myself, I felt disempowered. I was constantly struggling with the notion of being unapologetically me. I often felt that I had to shrink back so that others--family, spouse, friends, co-workers--wouldn't be uncomfortable with my grandeur. Society would have us believe that if we are unapologetic about ourselves, then we are being selfish or self-centered. This is the furthest from the truth! When we are unapologetic about who we are, we are simply saying, "I refuse to apologize for being me." That does not take anything away from anyone else, nor does it mean that you cannot be unapologetically you and still show up for others. This is a tough lesson to learn!

Learning to embody an unapologetic "F*ck That!" attitude is a journey that starts with three critical steps: 1) permission, 2) forgiveness and 3) believing

1. **Permission.** We have to give ourselves permission to start the journey. It seems like a really simple concept, right? However, it's not. You'd be surprised by how many people have never been given permission in their lives to do or be anything, let alone be themselves. I found that when we give ourselves permission, it let us know that it's ok. It's self-approval! It validates and affirms our needs. Permission includes granting ourselves grace as we embark on this new journey. Whenever we begin something new, it's inevitable that we may make some mistakes. THAT'S OK! Just give yourself permission to keep going. So, starting right now...give yourself permission to be YOU!

2. **Forgive ourselves for not living unapologetically.** Earlier in the book, I reminded us of the importance of forgiving ourselves. It's so important that I needed to address it twice. Remember, forgiving ourselves is the beginning of the healing process. In order to live unapologetically, we must forgive ourselves.

3. **Believe that we deserve to have what we want!** You, I, we DESERVE it! Whatever it is our hearts desire, we have a right to have it! Decide what you want. Believe you can have it. Believe you deserve it and believe it's possible for you. We are so much more powerful than we give ourselves credit for. Time to let go and change our negative, self-defeating thoughts into those that exude belief for what you deserve.

Don't worry about failing or making a mistake! Because sometimes we will, and that's OK. Besides, failing or making a mistake produces the most significant growth! Just don't get stuck because when you get stuck, you shrink!

Morning Cup of F! That! with Coffee...
Thank You, Jesus, for reminding me how important it is to be true to MYSELF - no matter what that is AND/OR even if it changes from day to day! Thank You for giving me the strength to do what I believe, and feel is right for ME, even when others disagree and/or do not understand! Most of us live a life by the design of others- spouses, kids, partners, parents, bosses, friends, enemies, society, culture, religion, etc. And when we do, we allow them to dictate OUR path. As a result, we end up conflicted because we're trying to do something that is so unnatural to our spirits. We're denying our true selves. So, we fight and struggle internally, remaining miserable until we begin doing what we know is right for us. My Beloved, we cannot live the life that others want us to live! We have to follow our

guide, our inner voice/gut feeling no matter how much others may try to prevent us from doing so. Having the courage to be bold enough to step out on faith and move through fear, judgment and criticism is how it begins. Have enough belief in yourself to know and do what's best for YOU, even if you sometimes have to do it alone! But remember you're never truly alone! God is always with us! And those who genuinely love us will encourage us, even if they don't understand. And if they don't, F*ck'em! Our joy comes first and that begins by being unapologetically true to self!

CHAPTER 7
F! THAT!!!

Over the years, throughout the process of learning to say, "F! That!" and writing this book, I've relearned what it really means to live unapologetically! This point was driven home by a very powerful video I watched recently. The video reverberated an earth-shattering truth in my spirit. The gentleman being interviewed in the video was speaking about various topics, but one particular topic really caught my attention: death. The interviewer asked him if he was afraid of dying. The man being interviewed eloquently stated, "No, I do not fear death. I embrace it. The knowledge that I'm going to one day die creates the focus for the kind of life that I want to live today." That was extremely powerful! It resonated in my spirit! It helped to put so many things into perspective! My Beloved, we live life as if we're going to live forever. As if we're promised tomorrow. We're not! No one knows the hour in which we shall depart from this life. We waste soooo much time on things, people, places, jobs, and situations that are irrelevant! For what? Man... F! That! I don't want to live like that! I want to live with a sense of urgency! I don't want to waste my time left on this Earth waiting for tomorrow. It may never come. Also, I'm not going to live my life in a box, being who others think I should be! I'm going to live authentically --whatever that is for me! I don't know when my time will come, but I absolutely refuse to waste what's left! I'm going to live, laugh, and leave a lasting legacy that will score a victory for humanity! I will not die ashamed of never living the life that I wanted to live! So, when you see me living it up, join in, or please step aside and continue to wait for your tomorrow.

Just like you, my Beloved, I am trying very hard to be who I am meant to be! Taking an internal look into the depth from which your life springs requires courage, strength, trust, transparency, and afterwards it requires an unapologetic audacity, boldness, and an "F! That!" attitude wrapped in humility and grace!

My Beloved, this life is incredibly beautiful! "F! That!" You and I deserve to experience that life unapologetically!

APPENDIX A
MORNING CUPS OF F! THAT! WITH COFFEE

When You Don't Feel Normal

Morning Cup of F! That! with Coffee...
I am so glad that I'm NOT normal! What the heck is "normal" anyway? Normal is a bunch of BS; a "standard" that society has deemed acceptable to make others feel comfortable while isolating anything that is different. Normal is a statistical average that ignores the beautiful diversity of life. It's a very narrow path that fails to allow for any deviation. Normal polices anything that doesn't fit perfectly into societal, familial, cultural, spiritual, political, etc. expectations...norms. These norms convince people that they are emotionally unbalanced because of their lifestyle choices that dare to be different. But the crazy thing about it is that these so-called norms change all the time based on any given number of reasons. Trying to keep up and fit in with norms only creates internal disharmony and chaos. That's why it's so much better to just be yourself! My Beloved, we have to begin to challenge normal! The construct of this notion of normal breeds pathology by which others use to diagnose. Who wants to abide by a guideline that creates a space for non-tolerance, judgement, and violence? Who wants to be a clone of society's fear of life? Who wants to be normal when there are so many beautiful colors to life? Who wants to be normal when "normal" is based on the fallacy of reality. Who wants to be normal when it's just so much easier to be you! Not this chick! F! being normal! I'm not interested in normal--It's not my goal! I DARE to be different! I dare to live a life that is not confined to beliefs, judgment, or stigma that is held in place by elitist, privileged folks who lack the gumption to challenge conventional notions. I refuse to blend into the monotony of life by allowing normal to neutralize my creativity and box in my exceptionality. Trust and believe, this life ain't for the faint at heart, but I'd rather live life unrefined than to be sucked into the stereotypical and safe path of normal! Y'all can keep your "normal!" That's just not me...

When You Need To Face Your Fear

Morning Cup of F! That! with Coffee...
I'm so grateful that I've learned to use my fear as fuel. At times, I have allowed my fears to prevent me from doing things I really wanted to do and things I knew I should've done. As a result, I've missed soooo many wonderful opportunities and experiences. I also missed some amazing people because of fear. Fear can be debilitating. It keeps us stuck and

stagnant by disguising itself as many things such as: stress, loneliness, depression, worry, anxiety, etc. Fear is so good that it even appears in the form of a friend, a partner, a parent, a spouse, a family member, etc. Fear is one of the best techniques used by satan to prevent us from living, taking chances, enjoying life and doing God's work. If we're afraid of something, we're less likely to do it. Now of course it's natural to wonder about the unknown but to allow our fears to paralyze us, is to prevent us from moving forward to becoming all we are meant to be. My Beloved, it's time to face our fears. Square up, look your fears in the face and "say it with your chest" F! you {insert fear here}!" And continue naming each and every one! Tell your fears to "pack yo' -ish and get out! I no longer can or will allow you to stop me from living my life as I choose to or from fulfilling my God given Purpose!" Y'all know that God did not give us a spirit of fear but rather one of love right? And so, shall we move forth in love allowing faith and hope to be our guide. Oh! And one last thing, moving forth in love does not mean- doing everything or anything that "they" approve of! Moving forth in love means that you honor your needs, wants, and desires first! And that doesn't mean you don't love "them," it just means you love yourself more and enough not to be miserable and controlled by fear!

When You Need To Make A Decision

Morning Cup of F! That! with Coffee..

Thank You, Jesus, for keeping me as I grow in my capacity to make decisions! It's said that Jesus watches over babies and fools. Well, I know for certain that it must be true because man...I have made some crazy decisions. I have gotten myself into some situations that only a baby or fool would get into! The only way I survived is simply because He kept me! You see the process of keeping is two-fold. God does His part, but we also have a part to do! Our part is to learn and grow from our situations. It's to become wise and discerning. When we fail to learn our lesson, we end up in the same ole crazy -ish over and over again. And then we wonder why God "let" this happen. Uhm...it's not God or anyone else, it's us! We have to stop blaming our random foolishness on others...God included. We have to learn to put our big girl panties on and big boy drawers on and become accountable for our -ish! You see society doesn't teach us accountability. It teaches us to point the finger at everything and everyone else except ourselves. What kind of -ish is that? Oh! It's the kind of -ish that stinks! It's the kind of -ish that fools only ourselves and oh yeah it's the kind of "-ish otherwise known as a false perception of self. My Beloved! It's time to grow the up and start making decisions that reflect wisdom and maturity. When we are young, we speak and do as children. F that! I don't have time for childish decisions because I'm not a child anymore.

When You Need Motivation About Your Purpose

Morning Cup of F! That! with Coffee...
I'm not scared to do what I've been chosen to do!! Man... I've been chosen to talk about, speak on, advocate for, and educate others on some powerful, life changing, stigmatizing, judgmental, misunderstood, taboo - ish...SEXUALITY!! I answered The Call over 25 years ago and I'm so glad I did, because there's nothing else in this entire world that I'd rather do! But please believe that doesn't mean it's easy! I get all sort of push back, crazy looks, fear, doubt, shaming, and judgment because people's conceptual framing of sexuality has been so skewed by so many different factors! But that's alright! I welcome the closed minds, the lack of understanding, the scrutiny and all of the challenges that come with it because it's an opportunity for me to educate and empower! It's an opportunity to change lives! Another thing that I've learned about the work that I've been called to do, is that MY brand of sexuality is not the popular message because I talk about the tough stuff! My brand is not so much focused on sexual pleasure! Of course, I could talk about pleasure! Orgasms! Positions! I could present half-naked, make sexual gestures, or be overtly sexual to get my point across or sell sex but that's the surface part of sexuality! And besides, we're already over sexualized and under educated and I refuse to contribute to or be a part of the unhealthy societal framing of sexuality. - We got more than enough of that! I'd rather focus on saving lives by providing individuals with comprehensive information, knowledge and skills to make safer and informed decisions! Safety, sane, consensual, responsibility and accountability are not always popular! But it's all good!! F! That! I don't do this -ish for likes! For followers! I do this to save lives! The work I do...ain't for everybody! My Beloved, what have you been Chosen to do? Have you answered The Call? God has given you a specific gift that only you can fulfill so what are you waiting for? Don't let fear, doubt and "they" stop you from answering your call! Jesus is on the mainline...pick up! Or maybe He's posting or messaging you on Facebook, "if you got this call hit amen" LOL But for real, for real...answer The Call! Let Jesus use you, change the world and leave a lasting legacy! And whatever you do, do it with integrity, stay true to what you have been chosen to do, don't water down your brand or message and don't sell your soul just for a like or following!

When You Are Dealing With The Unknown

Morning Cup of F! That! with Coffee ...
It's so funny how we think we know ourselves until that very moment that someone or something challenges us rocking our very existence to the core! It's in that moment that we begin to question, doubt and maybe even fear

everything that we thought we knew about ourselves. Man... is that ever a F'ed up yet amazing place to be because it stretches us! It forces us to face our -ish! It forces us to make a decision! It provides an opportunity for growth! The true essence of knowing ourselves involves understanding that what we know about ourselves is susceptible and vulnerable to the unknown at any given time. Knowing ourselves also involves realizing that no matter how much we try to anticipate our responses to people, situations and experiences, we never really know how we'll respond until we know in that very moment. So then how do we move? We do so by not trying to predict the future but rather by embracing the present and embodying the moment. F! trying to figure it all out because we don't have to! All we have to do is live and take life as it comes. We'll never fully know ourselves and such is the beauty and colors of life! Learn to embrace the unknown and pray for the strength to move through it gracefully and lovingly. Because the one thing that we know for sure is that life is full of the unknown...who knew! Lol

When You Need To Walk Away

Morning Cup of F! That! with Coffee...
Sometimes you just have to walk away! Walking away from someone or something that you love (or think you love) can be one of the most difficult things to do! You feel like you're giving up on your dreams, hopes, and desires. You feel like you're letting go of something or someone that is so near and dear to your heart! You feel like you've invested your all, only to walk away. It hurts like hell! You feel like a failure! And some days, you just don't even feel like going on. I know! I've resided in this place more than enough times in my life to know that walking away is not always easy, but sometimes it's necessary! Sometimes it's the only thing you can do, especially when the relationship is not healthy, the person is not treating you the way you want to be treated, the person no longer wants to be with you, even though you want them, and/or you've outgrown them and the relationship. Unfortunately, there's no handbook to tell you how, where or when enough is enough. Only you will know that! But trust and believe when you finally reach that point where you're no longer willing to question or sacrifice your worth, your peace, your sanity, yourself...My Beloved it's time to walk! Cut the strings, stop dangling like a puppet, pack up your self-worth and your ish and move the F! on! Don't look back! Just keep walking into the greater blessings that are in store for you! F! trying to hold on to someone or something that's not meant to be! It's too exhausting and it takes waaaay too much energy and time! And besides, I don't have time to be out here in these streets looking crazy and desperate trying to hold on to something that's not good for me or someone who doesn't want me!

When You're Trying To Make Sense Of A Situation

Morning Cup of F! That! with Coffee...

Thank God I've learned the difference between situations that I ordained versus situations that God ordained. Often, we find ourselves in situations (or marriages, relationships, careers) that we believe God ordained, when in reality, it's a situation that we *want* to be in because we think it's cute; we want to have a wedding; it's the "right" thing to do; we want to impress them, they and the others; the pay is good; we don't want to be alone; we have too much pride or fear to walk away; and all that other foolish -ish we tell ourselves or believe to justify "our" decision to stay in a BS situation! Meanwhile, deep down inside we're dying, trying to save face because we're too concerned about what "others" will think. After all, "it" was ordained by God, right? Wrong! Just because you're in it, doesn't mean that God ordained it! Maannnn...F! That! My Beloved, you gotta know the difference! We gotta stop using the belief that God ordained it as a justification or an excuse to make ourselves feel better about staying in some F*ed up situations! Look here, God didn't ordain half (well, probably most) of the situations we're in or that we get into! Stop blaming God for our human f*ups! He doesn't supersede our free will! It's time to be honest with ourselves, put on our big girl panties or big boy drawers, boss up and make an adult decision! So gon' ahead and exercise your free will today!

When You Need To Believe In Love

Morning Cup of F! That! with Coffee...

Today I am so grateful that even in a crazy world, I still believe in love! This 4-letter word, powerful it is! Love, one of the world's most sought after emotions. One of the most frequently misunderstood and misused terms! An action verb often imitated by some cheap knock-off version. Conditionally unconditional but yet TRUE love perfects all! Love its patient in our impatience. Love never dies, it just changes from one form to another. We just have to learn to recognize its differences. I believe in loves miraculous healing powers. Powers that can heal a shattered & scattered broken heart. For love does not fail us we fail love, belittle love, mistreat love when it does not become what we so selfishly desire. We turn our backs on love blaming it for our random transgressions and indiscretions. Love cannot be bought or sold, manipulated or contrived, held tight out of fear. Love is freedom to be just as we are! It soars with an Angels glow; on the wings of love we grow! I believe in love and its ability to transform lives as I have seen it at work in mines. I strive to walk within love's ecstatic state; beyond the world of limitations into the world of boundlessness! But in order to ascend; for love to work we must not be afraid to risk being vulnerable enough to open our hearts, forgive, let go & let God! For He is LOVE! HE-IS-LOVE! And the greatest of these...is LOVE!! F! everything else, I'm all about LOVE!

Thank You, Jesus, for love! Love is real! To experience it is surreal! Love is one of the world's most sought after yet misunderstood emotions! It's over used and underrated! People will do some crazy things all for the sake of or in the name of love. Over the years, I have loved and lost and loved and lost again! Each and every time, I loved I believed it was real regardless of the outcome. What I took away from each dance with love was intense, raw, and real! Not once did I ever question love, I questioned myself because I was the common denominator in all of the experiences. And you know what? I figured out that I had this love thing all wrong. I was living in the illusion of love. What I learned is that we really don't understand the true essence of love. Love is not this made up superficial emotion that Hollywood has sold us for years! It's not some feeling that makes our heart skip a beat! It's not a verb that we base someone's actions on. Here's the heavy part...love is definitely not comfortable! Contrary to popular belief, love is very uncomfortable! Ask Jesus! He died on the cross all because He loved us! He suffered all because He loved us! He dealt with the hate and judgment of others all because He loved us! The essence of love is the ability to endure! It's strength! It's the ability to prevail against all odd! It's the power to overcome and RISE again! That's love! It's an undying, unstoppable energy that is transferred from one to another. My Beloved we can't transfer something we do not truly embody. At best we're transferring some watered-down misconception that we've mistaken for love. In order to truly experience love in all its essence, we have to first embody love for ourselves. If we don't, we merely transfer our "-ish to someone else, get mad at them and/or end up hurt. The funny part is that we then swear that love does not exist or that it's not real. Well my Beloved it's not that love is not real or does not exist, we just failed to find it in ourselves first. What we can't find in ourselves, we damn sure can't find in others! And to lay to rest that whole fallacy about falling "in love" ...it doesn't exist! And besides, who wants to fall into anything? F that! I want to live love 365 days a year! There's nothing else I'd rather do than love! And ahhh! It feels so good!

When You Must Tell People To Stay Out Of Your Business

It's such a shame that I have to say this, but I will! And this will be my first and last time saying it! Look here...if you have a question or concern about something that I post on MY page, then ask ME! You don't have to call, send a text, message, send a smoke signal or whatever to anybody else asking them *anything* about what I post! I'm very capable of answering any question that you may have! Not only is it messy as hell to look at someone's post, make an assumption, and then run off and tell someone else, it's also very presumptuous to think that you have the right to check me! Get the F! out of here! I'm grown--over 40 plus years grown! I say what I want, when I want, and how I want! I don't have to justify it to anyone! And besides, if you're really that concerned, then ask ME! So again, I say if you have a question, comment, concern, etc. about what I post, then ASK ME! Now go run tell that! And by the way...good morning!

When You Need To Be Reminded About What Truly Matters

Morning Cup of F! That! with Coffee...
Yup, I finally got the message! I just hope others will too! We better stop wasting time, energy focus and love on people, things and situations that really don't matter...because the one thing that's for damn sure is that life is not promised! F! tomorrow, you better honor each moment and opportunity! Start spending more time with and focusing on people that truly love you, things that are positive, and situations that build you! Oh, and save the bull -ish tired ass excuses on why we can't or how busy we are because the moment something happens, we wanna start slanging snot and crying about how much we loved them, how it meant or how we'd do things differently! Or we want to act like that person, situation or thing was super important to us!! Save it! If your loved ones, things, situations are really that important and really matter that much, tell them TODAY!! Show it NOW!! Waiting until our loved one is casket sharp and/or situations and things are destroy is useless! Real fact...you don't have the rest of your life to make it right, so take that opportunity NOW! Now for the gut check...to all those things that don't matter, they're replaceable! For all those unhealthy situations...deuces! And lastly to those of you who play with your words by saying you love me and mean me well but really don't, hear me loud and clear when I say...move the F! on, get the F! out of my life! K! I'm tired of you taking up time and space from people who really love me! If you have to wonder if I'm talking to you, don't wonder...I am! This moment forth...I'm spend my moments with people, things and situations that really matter! My LIFE, my time, my energy, my focus, my love is waaaay to important to waste.

When You Need To Be Reminded That You Are Fearfully And Wonderfully Made

Morning Cup of F! That! with Coffee ...
Today I'm so grateful for being able to accept and be myself. I'm a eclectic, eccentric, non-traditional, edgy, quirky, giddy, girlie, abstract, colorful and even a little weird; nevertheless it's me! I'm different! I accept it and I love it! It's definitely been a journey to get to this point but thank God I have! And even though I'm able, it is a continuous process to maintain. Many people are afraid to live their authentic self because of fear, shame or rejection. It takes a bold person to keep showing up and putting themselves out there. It takes courage not to undermine and betray who we really are instead of searching for approval from others. It's only when we are able to accept ourselves that others will accept us. We must be able to love ourselves before we can attract the love we desire. And in order to do so, we must go to The Source of love. My Beloved, we must continue to walk in and breathe in The Source of love by opening your heart to being grateful and receiving all that God has for us. We must not be afraid to walk through the fire in order to come forth as pure gold! Let's no longer be apologetic for who we are! For we are fearfully and wonderfully made!

When You Need Self-Control

Morning Cup of F! That! with Coffee...
Thank you for self-control! Man... I swear sometimes I just want to snap the F off! But before I do, I stop and ask myself ...TaMara...how beneficial is this to the quality of your life? I also ask myself what I hope to gain by snapping. Will I feel good because I just told "them" off or will I just look ignorant and immature, like an idiot. The latter is usually the case. See the difference between snapping/popping off/reacting and responding is that responding is all about demonstrating self-control. Whereas reacting lacks self-control. It's easy to fly off the handle, pop off and snap! That doesn't take much brainpower at all! It's an animalistic urge. But responding is a fruit of the spirit! It takes much more discipline and effort to control yourself. Unfortunately, society doesn't teach us to control ourselves. The societal norm is to show out and act a damn fool when things aren't going our way, when we don't get what we want or when we feel disrespected. This behavior is evident by all the violence and such that we see on television, hear in music, and see posted on social media. My Beloved we have to learn how to maintain self-control! YES, our emotions can be a beast! TRUST, I know!! And YES, emotions tend to get the best of us sometimes. But learning how to pause, take a breath, and wait a second before responding, not reacting, is absolutely essential! It can make all the

difference in the world; like life or death difference. Look, I'm not trying to end up laying down all because I could not effectively maintain control of myself. Life is too short for that BS! F! That! I don't care what "they" say orange is NOT the new black! Please believe me! Orange is NOT my color!

When You Feel The Need To Cry

Morning Cup of F! That! with Coffee...
Thank you for my tears! I am such a crier! I will cry at the drop of a dime! And depending on the day, moment or experience, it doesn't take much to make me tear up. Each and every tear that falls serves a purpose! Whether it is to heal my spirit, to mend my scattered and shattered broken heart or whether it is to celebrate a joyous occasion or because I'm blown away by a romantic notion, it's all necessary! It's what I need! Society has taught us that for whatever reason, we -especially men/boys- shouldn't cry and if we do it's a sign of weakness or vulnerability. It's like how dare we show emotion and especially in front of someone. So instead, we cry in silence behind closed doors; in solitude. Look here, that's some ole bull -ish! F! that! Stop telling people not to cry! We cry because we're experiencing some type of emotion. We have emotions because we're human. So... how could we not do something that is so very natural for humans? Get the F! outta here! My Beloved, sometimes you've gotta cry! I'm talking about a good ole snot dripping, dry heaving, barely breathing, ugly cry! You know like Viola Davis in Fences! LOL Seriously though, we've gotta release the stress, tension and pressure that's built up and sometimes a good ole cry is the best way. Sometimes it's the only way to move forward. So, whatever it is let it go today! Cry! Scream! Holler! Get it out! It's ok! Who gives a damn who's looking! Cleanse your soul and heal your spirit! I promise you'll feel better! I know I always do!

When You Need A Reminder To Honor Yourself

Morning Cup of F! That! with Coffee...
Thank you for reminding me how important it is to be true to MYSELF - no matter what that is AND/OR even if it changes from day to day! Thank You for giving me the strength to do what I believe, and feel is right for ME, even when others disagree and/or do not understand! Most of us live a life by the design of others- spouses, kids, partners, parents, bosses, friends, enemies, society, culture, religion, etc. And when we do, we allow them to dictate OUR path. As a result, we end up conflicted because we're trying to do something that is so unnatural to our spirits. We're denying our true selves. So, we fight and struggle internally, remaining miserable until we

begin doing what we know is right for us. My Beloved, we cannot live the life that others want us to live! We have to follow our guide, our inner voice/gut feeling no matter how much others may try to prevent us from doing so. Having the courage to be bold enough to step out on faith and move through fear, judgment and criticism is how it begins. Have enough belief in yourself to know and do what's best for YOU; even if you sometimes have to do it alone! But remember you're never truly alone! God is always with us! And those who genuinely love us will encourage us, even if they don't understand. And if they don't F*ck'em! Our joy comes first and that begins by being unapologetically true to self!

When You Need Saving From Yourself

Morning Cup of F! That! with Coffee...
Thank You, Jesus, for saving me from myself! Whew! There was a time in my life when I thought I wanted him! I thought I needed him! I thought I loved him! I just had to have him! I tried evvvvvverything in my human power to make the relationship work. But no matter what I did, how I did it or even what I said, things just did not work out. At the time it was very disappointing, heartbreaking and hurtful because I wanted it so bad or at least I thought I did! But as I look back over the experience with new eyes, I can smile! I even laugh because had I gotten what I thought I wanted, I'd certainly be an unhappy miserable mess! But thank God, He knew better! Thank God He saved me from me! My Beloved, God is trying to save you from yourself! Who or what is He trying to save you from? We all have made plenty of questionable decisions and even loved some questionable and undeserving people. But the beautiful thing about it all is that, it's all over! It's in the past! It's time to say F! that, let it go and walk away! We must forgive ourselves, do the work to heal and move on! God saved us this time! So, shall we learn from the experience and/or situation because the next time... we might not be saved! And besides look at it this way, he, she, they or it turned out to be the best thing we never had!

When You've Hit Rock Bottom

Morning Cup of F! That! with Coffee...
Thank You, Jesus, for rock bottom! I hit rock bottom -hard- in 2006 when I found myself laying on the bathroom floor, next to the toilet, curled up in a ball, crying uncontrollably while my then ex-husband stood over me yelling at the top of his lungs *"Hurt! Hurt! Now you know how pain feels"* As I laid there for what seemed like forever, his snarky, arrogant voice faded into the background like the adults on the Charlie Brown cartoons. Although I don't

remember much, I do remember wondering how in the hell did I get here? How in the hell did I let this man, my husband, abuse me in this way? I was supposed to be this "empowered, college educated, Christian woman." I was "supposed to know better." But yet... here I am at my lowest point in my life, contemplating my life. Rock bottom is a haaaard place to be! You feel alone, embarrassed, and ashamed. You question and wonder why me Lord? Hitting rock bottom hurts like hell! You feel numb; like you can't make it; like you no longer want to go on. But God! See even in the midst of everything I was going through, I still held on to my mustard seed of faith...NOT my religion but my relationship!! That's what saved me! That's what helped me realize why I hit rock bottom and why not me! It had to be me, so I could share my story with others so that it may empower, strengthen, or give voice to an otherwise hurting and lost soul...just like me! My Beloved, have you hit rock bottom? Trust me, it's ok! But now it's time to dust yourself off and get up. For you were built for a time such as this! Glean in the moment and revel in the Blessing! Rock bottom is exactly where we need to be sometimes because it's the only place where we can look up and see all the amazing opportunities, experiences and Blessings in our LIFE! And it's also the place where God can get our undivided attention. F! that! I would not change my experience for anything in the world! I thank God I hit rock bottom because now I know what it feels like to be up!! And I'm waaaaaaay up! I feel Blessed! I know how Big Sean, Drake and Kanye feel! YES!!! I'm living my L.I.F.E. way up! Live Inspired Feel Empowered.

When You Need Faith

Morning Cup of F! That! with Coffee...

Thank You, Jesus, for reminding me how Great Thy Faithfulness is! Lord You have always been there for me! You have always been faithful to me even when I have not been faithful to You! I know I don't deserve it, but Your Grace, Mercy and Favor always abounds; through the good AND the bad! It's easy to be faithful when things are going good and life seems wonderful! In those moments, we're way up and feeling ourselves! But let me tell you when that woom doom comes down and that so unnecessary hits us and stress, frustration and worry kicks in man...do we ever get to back pedaling, questioning and even acting a fool. It gets so hard that sometimes we want to give up. But in those times, we must also be faithful! As challenging as it may be, we still need to be steadfast, unmovable, always abounding in His Work! Once we truly embody this, we can breathe easier and relax because we know no matter what, He's got us! My Beloved, the one thing I know for sho is that God is Faithful! He never, not ever fails us! We fail ourselves because we get in our own way. We expect God to operate in our time and when He doesn't we lose faith. But here's the thing, that's our fault...not Gods. F! That! Stop blaming God and others for our lack of faith. We must be accountable for our own faithfulness. Trust I know it's not easy! But it's not impossible! It requires discipline, practice and work! Remember faith without works is dead. And here's another thing, if we are not faithful with what God has already given us not only are we in danger of losing what we already have; why in the world would He Bless us with more? So today, check your faithfulness! Is it lacking? Are you being a good steward over what you've already been given? What has you all bent outta shape, angry, torn, or feeling like you just don't know? Whatever it is, I encourage you to activate your faithfulness. Be confident in the fact that whatever He has laid on your heart will come to pass! He placed it there for a reason! All you have to do is be faithful and rest assure. God will reward your faithfulness! When we are faithful over a few things, He will make us ruler over many.

When You Need To Focus

Morning Cup of F! That! with Coffee...
Thank You, Jesus, for teaching me to focus! When a horse runs a race, it has on a blinder. The purpose of the blinder is to keep the horse from looking at what's going on around them and to keep them focus on what's in front of them as they run their race. Focus or the lack there of is one of the major reasons why we experience the things we do. The meaning and significance of each experience, each situation is determined by how much focus we put into it. Our focus creates our future. Therefore, we must keep our minds fixed on whatever it is we so desire. Whatever we focus on today, we give permission to exist tomorrow. Focus and faith are closely related. In order to accomplish what you desire, you first have to be able to see it. Focus makes your faith unshakable, helps to eliminate distractions and allows us to move forward with purpose. If you do not want to see something in your future do not focus on it from this day forth. Train your mind to focus on the positive and you will receive positive outcomes. My Beloved, where's your focus? It's time to put your blinder on and go hard for all that you desire! Do not allow anyone or anything to alter your focus! F! worrying or focusing on other people and other things! We have to be so focused on running our own race that we don't have the time to focus on anyone or anything else! I don't know about y'all but...umm I'm focusing on all the dreams that God has placed in my heart! And with persistence and passion I shall proceed and succeed! I'm focused man! #yup #unapologetic #winning

When You Need To Prioritize

Morning Cup of F! That! with Coffee...
I'm so thankful that I've learned to prioritize. On any given day there are so many things pulling us in different directions, work, family, etc. We overbook, over commit and over extend ourselves way beyond our capacity. When we do we barely have time left for ourselves to focus on ourselves and what we really need or want to do. We get so tangled up in a web of deadlines and obligations and we end up burnt out. Our schedules are so crammed with "busy" that we don't have enough time and space for God and ourselves. The discipline of prioritizing prevents entanglement and stress. It helps to create boundaries, space and time. It frees your mind and heart to focus on and manifest the Divine. The highest priority is NOT to focus on what others are doing but rather to always stay connected to the Presence of the Divine and to listen to His still small voice for guidance. Life is adventure full of excitement, plans, opportunities, and implementation but too many irons in the fire can eventually put out the fire. The key is not to prioritize what's on your schedule but to schedule your priorities. My Beloved who and/or what is a priority in your life? Our challenge today is to identify them and place them in their proper perspective. Let's not give a person, place, relationship or thing the power of priority in our lives especially when or if we're just the option! F! That! Never forget YOU, I, WE are a priority!

When You're Going Through A Storm

Morning Cup of F! That! with Coffee...
Thank You, Jesus, I didn't give up! Man... there have been so many times in my life when I just felt like I just couldn't make it. I didn't know what to do. I wanted to give up! But just when I did, God stepped in and said hold on baby girl, I'm your way out if you just let it go, depend on, open your heart and give your life to me, I got you! He made a way out of no way! The impossible became possible! The invisible appeared! The stormy winds and rains faded into a colorful rainbow! You can trust and believe that I've been clinging to His promise and holding on to His unchanging hand ever since! Sometimes and some days it can be a little more challenging than others but nevertheless I don't give up! And besides, F! That! I'm not a quitter any way! My Beloved, this day I say to you hold out, help is on the way! Don't give up! Continue to pray! God hears you! He really does! He's just working it out in your best interest. And His Timing is EVERYTHING!!! So...at this very moment, let go, turn it over to Him, open your heart, allow patience and faith to have its perfect works! Breathe! And get ready for your rainbow!

When You Need To Surrender

Morning Cup of F! That! with Coffee...
I'm so glad I have surrendered! The power of surrendering is so Freeing! When you surrender, you can soar! Life becomes a truly amazing experience! Surrendering is NOT giving up! It's total trust and faith in the process of life! It's knowing that ALL things work together for the good for those who love HIM and are called according to HIS Purpose! When you truly embody this, then you can surrender because you KNOW that God has got you no matter what! You don't have to fight. You don't have to complain. You don't have to worry. You don't have to compete. You don't have to stress. You don't have to frown. You don't let what others say control you. You don't live for man! You can breathe! You can embrace change! You can relax! You can smile! You can chill! My Beloved, F! The fight...just surrender! JUST surrender...

When You Need To Embrace Your Imperfections

Morning Cup of F! That! with Coffee...
Thank you for my imperfections! It hasn't always been easy to accept my imperfections. However, over the years, I have learned to embrace, honor and appreciate my imperfections! They make me human! They make me unique! They make me dope! Often times when we look in the mirror, we immediately focus on all our blemishes, scars, weight, hair, etc. - our flaws, our imperfections. And because we feel some type of way about our imperfections, we try to cover them up or fix them with makeup, waist trainers, hair systems, belching cream, implants, eye lashes, crazy diets, surgeries, etc. We spend soooo much money, time and effort trying to capture perfect! However, what we fail to realize is that even after trying and/or using all of that stuff, the imperfections are still there. All we did was conceal them for a moment. This ideal of "imperfect" is a tired ass mind set. We must change our mind in order to really change our imperfections. My Beloved, we must love ourselves imperfections and all! The notion of being perfect is some ole bull -ish that society has sold us for so long! No matter how much we try, we will never fit that definition of "perfect." It's unrealistic and unattainable! It's not really for us anyway! And truthfully no matter what "they" say, no one on this Earth is perfect, no matter how much "they" try to pretend! It's time to face yourself in the mirror and begin to dismantle the construction of perfection! So, as we move on today facing ourselves in the mirror let's say; "mirror, mirror on the wall, I love myself flaws and all! I may not be perfect but imperfect (Im perfect) as I am!" And besides ... F! perfection! It makes life boring anyway!

When You Need To Check Your "-ish

Morning Cup of F! That! with Coffee...
Thank You, Jesus, for the ability to check myself and own my -ish! We all have the ability to get out of order - with others and even ourselves- from time to time. Man... whew weeeee! There are times when I know that I am just allllll out of order! So occasionally throughout the day, I stop and check myself. Like I literally have to have a conversation with myself. I'm like "TaMara... girl ...you need to get yo -ish together because right now, you are alllll out of order right and it's not even cute." When we're out of order, we experience unnecessary drama and conflict in our daily interactions and relationships because of our -ish. This is why it's so important that we learn our triggers because it helps to minimize the drama and conflict in our lives. But more than that, it's also important that we're honest with ourselves and own our -ish no matter how foul it is or how difficult it is. We gotta grow up! My Beloved, we need to check ourselves! Believe it or not our -ish stinks! Yup, it does! It's not acceptable to have temper tantrums like children and fly off the handle just because we're having a bad day. F! That! BS excuse! Everyone has bad days, moments, experiences, etc. We're not special because of it! It doesn't give us the right to act a damn fool! We have to get our adult on! The beautiful thing about being an adult is that we possess the cognitive ability to control and regulate ...CHECK our attitudes and behaviors. So today when we start to find our -ish getting in the way, let's step back and take a moment to check ourselves before we wreck ourselves! Somebody cue Ice Cube please! HA!

When You Need A Reminder To Stop Comparing Yourself To Others

Morning Cup of F! That! with Coffee...
Thank You, Jesus, for MY LIFE! F! comparison! We spend so much time comparing our lives to the lives of others. We make sooooo many judgments and assumptions about "their" lives based on our perceptions. We wonder why "they" are successful and/or receiving blessings that we're not. We wonder why their life is going so easy. However, what we fail to realize is that we only have a slight view into their "perfect" Facebook, Instagram or Snapchat, etc. life. We really don't have a clue of what their real life is like or what it takes to maintain their life. We don't have an understanding of the sacrifice or struggle it took for them to get to where they are. We don't know why God has or is blessing them. And real talk, it's really not our business! And besides if we really knew their story, their struggle, their sacrifice, most of us couldn't handle it! I'd rather live the life I've been given. My Beloved stop comparing your life to others! If we spent more time living our lives and focusing on all the beautiful lessons and

blessings that God has in store for us, we'll begin to see monumental change in our lives. We must be grateful for what He has done for us because our lives could be changed in the twinkling of an eye. It is only by His Grace that we are who we are! Let's not be concerned with what God does for others but rather what we can do for God! And besides, God is more than able to provide more than enough for all of us! So... the next time someone else receives a blessing, instead of screwing up our face, let's be happy and congratulate them! It doesn't take anything away from us to celebrate someone else. Plus, you'd be surprised at how amazing you'll feel! And if we just hold out and play our position, we'll receive our Blessing(s) in due time!

When You Need A Reminder Not To Jump To Conclusions

Morning Cup of F! That! and Coffee...
I'm so thankful that I've learned not to assume and jump to conclusions. In the past, I had a habit of allowing my mind to wonder about how come, what if and why/why not? Man ... ...and by the time I was finished, I'd have a whole story made up in my mind based off some crazy ass assumptions that I made by overreacting and jumping to conclusions. What I've learned is that oftentimes things are not always what they seem. However, we create an alternate reality in our heads based on our own insecurities. And as if "real life" experiences aren't enough, social media has got us tripping so hard too! As soon as we see a post, pic, video, etc., here we go jumping to all sorts of conclusions because of course everything we see on Facebook, Twitter, Instagram, SnapChat, etc is real...right? My Beloved, we have to stop doing ourselves a disservice by making assumptions and jumping to conclusions! Assumptions create situations that do not exists by always expecting the worse. It causes unnecessary drama, conflict, emotional distress, torture, heartbreak...you name it! But the crazy part about all of this is that WE do it to ourselves because we allow our minds to assume instead of just asking questions. You know what they say about assuming right? Yup, assuming makes an ass out of you and (perhaps) me! Man ...F! assumptions!! I'd rather just ask the question to get the answer! I'd rather not place myself under some fictitious bondage as a result of allowing my mind to jump to conclusions! And besides, I'm too damn old and out of shape to be jumping to anything! But fa real though!

When You Need Faith

Morning Cup of F! That! with Coffee...

Tatted on my right shoulder is the Chinese symbol for faith. I got the tattoo in '96 because I had always considered myself to be a person of faith - and I thought it was cute too. But little did I know that one day an experience would write a check that my faith would have to cash! Now of course, up until that time my faith had been tested. But none of the previous experiences would test my faith like when I finally left my ex-husband. I did not have a clue about how I was going to make it! My rent was equal to one check, which at the time was $1,464. I was paid bi-weekly. So, that left me with $1,464 to pay my car note, auto insurance, renters insurance, utilities, cable, cell phone, gas, and other bills that accumulated as a result of the divorce. And oh yeah, I did have to eat too. I barely had enough money to make ends meet. But the truly crazy thing about it, is that I didn't care! I just knew that The Spirit told me to move and so I did. I stepped out on faith - without a question- and I praised God for the rest! All my bills were paid, my needs met and I even had a few things that I wanted. Most importantly, I had peace and joy! God rewarded me for my faithfulness. I thank Him soooooo much for that experience! It filled me up! My faith is tried and true! It's real and full of His promises! Was I scared? Heeeeeellll yeah, I was scared! However, because I was faithful to Him, I was able to do it afraid and He kept me! My Beloved, is your faith on full? If not, then you need to get a refill - in my Elle Varner voice! Faith without works is dead. When God calls us to task, we have to be ready to move, even if we are afraid! We cannot wait for God to reveal our next step before we move because that does not demonstrate our faith. When we learn to lean and trust in Him, we cannot go wrong. So, F! whatever is or has been holding you back! It's time to exercise your faith TODAY! God's got you! So uhm...what's holding you back now??

When You Need To Reminder That The Societal Script Was Not Written For You

Morning Cup of F! That! with Coffee...

Thank You, Jesus, for showing me that I didn't have to stick to the societal script! Societal scripts limit freedom, expression and pleasure! They are created and defined by groups and/or individuals and are used to silence, oppress and damage others; because those who created them are damaged themselves and/or because they are afraid to be who they are. As a result, we constantly measure ourselves or try to live up to some "standard" that has been forced on us. Control, judgement, conformity, etc. are mechanisms used by societal scripts to shame us into believing that anything that's outside or different than the societal script is abnormal. And who wants to be abnormal? So, we fall in line with the script so we won't be an outcast or ostracized. The real unfortunate thing is that even if it's killing us -literally and figuratively- we don't do anything about it. We stay in script! Man... look here! F! the societal script! Societal scripts are the death of exceptionalism and creativity. We cannot allow ourselves to be censored and silenced because of our desires to live a life that makes others uncomfortable. We must liberate ourselves from the "normative" societal script in order to save ourselves from a life of pain, shame, blaming! There's something so refreshing and brilliant in those who do not internalize societal norms but instead create their own path! When we embody and live out our own script, on our own terms, we are far healthier and more evolved than those who assimilate to the "norm." For we do not need more assimilation and immersion! We need radical rewriting of our current script! So... go get your pen and paper ready. It's time to create your own script and end scene! Because that current script wasn't created for you!

When You Need To Embrace The Unknown

Morning Cup of F! That! with Coffee...
I'm so grateful that I've learned to lean into the unknown! It's so funny how we think we know ourselves until that very moment that someone or something challenges us rocking our very existence to the core! It's in that moment that we begin to question, doubt and maybe even fear everything that we thought we knew about ourselves. Man... is that ever a F'ed up yet amazing place to be because it stretches us! It forces us to face our -ish! It forces us to make a decision! It provides an opportunity for growth! The true essence of knowing ourselves involves understanding that what we know about ourselves is susceptible and vulnerable to the unknown at any given time. Knowing ourselves also involves realizing that no matter how much we try to anticipate our responses to people, situations and experiences, we never really know how we'll respond until we know in that very moment. So then how do we move? Here's the thing, we do so by not trying to predict the future but rather by embracing the present and embodying the moment. F! trying to figure it all out because we don't have to! All we have to do is live and take life as it comes. We'll never fully know ourselves and such is the beauty and colors of life! Learn to embrace the unknown and pray for the strength to move through it gracefully and lovingly. Because the one thing that we know for sure is that life is full of the unknown...who knew?

When You Need Peace Of Mind

Morning Cup of F! That! with Coffee ...
Thank You, Jesus, for peace of mind! Over the years I have come to learn that there is nothing like having peace! It's priceless! But I'm not going to lie, as priceless as peace is sometimes it can definitely be a struggle to find and keep! Oftentimes we allow waaaay too many things, people, situations, etc. to interrupt our peace. And when we do all hell breaks loose and we begin to question and doubt everything, sometimes even our own existence. This is a very uncomfortable space to be in! It causes sadness, anxiety, depression, exhaustion, desperation, hopelessness, feelings of failure, suicidal ideology, etc. Our mind is sooooo powerful that it can create all sorts of situations! It can manifest chaos or it can manifest peace. It's all up to us! At any given time and in any given situation, the peace that we experience is totally within our control. It sounds easy right? But of course, that's not always the case. Trust I KNOW!! Do I ever KNOW! Yes, the struggle is real! Nevertheless, as challenging as it may be at times, it's not impossible. We still have the power to exercise mind over matter. We just have to dig deep and tap into our inner strength to channel it! My Beloved, I don't know about you but I'm all about peace! Y'all can have all that other -ish! My quality of LIFE is waaaay too important to compromise! So... if you're not about a peaceful life, then I can't with you! I will NOT with you! F! That!! I will no longer sacrifice my mind, my heart, my spirit, and my soul ...my peace! So please excuse me while I whoosah!

When You Need To Realize That You Can't Fix Other People

Morning Cup of F! That! with Coffee ...
I'm so grateful for being reminded that I can't! I can't fix you, change your ways, make you have a better attitude, help you be more positive or see the brighter side of things-especially when you don't want to. I can't convince you to leave or stay, change your mind, not to worrying, etc. I CAN'T! And trust...I will no longer try to! The only thing I CAN, is be ME! And the way I see it, if it's meant for you, then you'll get it! You'll change! You'll develop a better attitude and become more positive. You'll leave when you've had enough and/or you're ready. You'll stay if it's that what's important to you. You'll stop worrying when you're tired of being stressed the hell out. And when you begin to see things differently, you'll change your mind. All that is up to you, not me! This applies to spouses, lovers, friends, partners, family, children, siblings, co-workers, people driving in the lane next you...er'body!! My Beloved, you must know when you can't! You must accept the fact that no matter how totally amazing, great and/or wonderful we may be and no matter how much we want to help/save someone, there are just some

things we can't do. At the same time, we must also realize that this "can't" is not a reflection of us. When we become so engrossed and tied up in other folks and their stuff, we take away from the quality of our lives. While we're trying to be the "can" for others, we ultimately become the "can't" for ourselves and we suffer tremendously! F! That! I CAN'T! I know it! I own it! I embrace it! Hell …I'm celebrating it! My switch is flipped! It's one of the best things I've ever done for me! How'd I do it? I made a conscious decision to flip the switch! And beside I want to live the rest of my life in a space of peace! I can't do that trying to be someone else's can! Take that trash somewhere else! Nah baby, I'm not gonna be able to do it!

When You Need To Change Your Perspective

Morning Cup of F! That! with Coffee...
I'm so glad I was able to change my perspective! When I was in high school I adopted the mantra "expect the worst but hope for the best." As I look back now, that had to be the dumbest -ish ever! Like why would anyone want to expect the worst? Why would anyone want to draw that negativity to themselves...knowingly! That's crazy! What's even crazier is that I had the unmitigated gall to wonder why all these negatives things were happening to me. It was the worst! It never crossed my childish mind that the reason I was dealing with a lot of BS and receiving the worst is because "I" expected it. Duh! It's the basic law of attraction. Whatever we put out into the atmosphere is what we're likely to receive. So, I was only getting what I expected...THE WORSE! Whew! Thank God I grew up! As I have grown and experienced life, I've come to realize that I AM responsible for my thoughts and energy - my perspective- that I put out into the atmosphere. I draw unto myself those people, situations, experiences, etc. and I choose to draw love, light, peace and positivity! My Beloved, we have the power over perspective! When the power of the mind, law of attraction, positive intention and positive energy meet, our perspective on life, people, situations, experiences, etc. become beautiful! It's insane, to intentionally draw negative people, situations, experiences etc. to ourselves all because of our perspective. F! That... Life is too short to spend with the worst! I'm purposefully and intentionally moving with positive perspective! I'm kicking worst out! It can't live here! So, pack yo -ish and get out! You're absolutely not welcomed here anymore! Goodbye!

When You Need To Seize The Moment

Morning Cup of F! That! with Coffee...

I'm so grateful that I'm learning to seize the moment and take it for what it is! Often we look so far into situations that we can't even enjoy the moment. We get so caught up in trying to figure out what it's going to be that we miss out on what it is. This is especially true of our relationships. One thing I've realized is that the more we try to stir the pot adding too much seasoning, the saltier the soup begins to taste. In other words, trying to do too much can mess up an already good thing. And at the end of the day, no matter how much we stress, question, worry, cry, curse, scream and shout we still have to take it for what it is. My Beloved stop trying to figure it all out, right now! It is what it is and whatever it is, we must learn to respect and appreciate it. Let's learn to accept that things are the way they are for a certain reason that may be beyond our understanding at the time. Let's bask in the moment! Let's enjoy where we are and take it for what it is because these are moments in time that we will never ever get back. So, let's not waste our time on the bull -ish! F! That! I'm trying to taste, smell, touch, see and feel every moment! Carpe diem (seize the moment)...

When You Need To Survive The Meantime

Morning Cup of F! That's with Coffee...

Thank You, Jesus, for continuously helping me learn how to wait in the meantime. F! That! the meantime is hard! But what's even harder is learning how to wait in the meantime. That is without a doubt probably one of life's most difficult task. We are such a narcissistic generation of right now! We can be a little selfish and spoiled because we want what we want when we want it. We get so impatient and we try to force things and take matters into our own hands. When we do, we sometimes end up messing things up because we interfere with the natural flow of life. This makes the meantime worse because it creates more chaos and unnecessary challenges because we overthink, over analyze, worry, doubt, etc. We have to learn to allow life and time the opportunity to create the space for whatever it is we so desire. We must accept the fact that in due time we will get whatever it is we desire and if for whatever reason we do not then we have to learn to be OK with that too. My Beloved, how are you handling your meantime? If you're like me, at times it can be a struggle. The -ish is tough! But what I've learned is that the secret to surviving the meantime lies in finding something positive to shift your focus to. I know, I KNOW it's so much easier said than done! And honestly when you're in the meantime, that's the last -ish you wanna hear! I know I be like y'all can gone with that -ish! LOL but nevertheless, the truth always prevails and when we shift our focus, the meantime because more of a beautiful journey through life and everything else becomes less important. At the end of the day, we can't become so consumed by the meantime that we allow the gray areas to cloud our perspectives. We must learn to dance in the rain while waiting for the beautiful rainbow at the end of the storm. I'm turning on my favorite song to dance to right now.

When You Need To F! Protocol

Morning Cup of F! That! with Coffee...
I'm so grateful that I've learned that there's no one path that is definitively "right" --whatever the hell that is! Just because society, family, friends, spouses, or partners have given us a road map for what "they" believe success is, doesn't mean we have to follow it! Sometimes we have to break protocol and create our own set of rules to live by. We have to create our own paths to accomplishing whatever we want to accomplish! Who says there's only one path that leads to success- whatever the hell that is or however you define it. There are many different paths to reaching our destination(s)! It's all about finding the one that works for YOU! What works for you may not necessarily work for anyone else. New paths can be created every day! As long as we have breath in our bodies, we can make a way. We just have to step outside the box, tap into our authenticity and creativity and break protocol! My Beloved, F! Protocol! Sometimes we just have to buck the system, push back on the ordinary to become the extraordinary! We have to embrace our fluidity by creating our own path and following our own protocol! The beautiful thing about it all is that life creates space and freedom for us to navigate outside the lines of protocol. What are you waiting for? As for me, I'm building an empire with a solid foundation (God) that's resilient enough to withstand the test of time. I'm creating a legacy that leaves footprints forever embedded in the hearts and minds of those I love and serve. I'm sharing an unconditional and unconventional love that will transcend space and time and can only be defined as Divine. Will you join in this journey with me? If so, you gotta be bold and courageous enough to look protocol in the face and say F! YOU! I know I'm destined for greatness...

When You Need To Embrace Discomfort

Morning Cup of F! That! with Coffee...
I've learned to lean into the discomfort! Comfort can be a dangerous thing! It can squeeze the life out of us! When we are too comfortable, we allow ourselves to settle for things, people and situations that aren't necessarily good for us. When we're comfortable, we're more likely to sit in the midst

of the foolishness, no matter how crazy it is, because it's what we're used to. It's what we know. We'd rather operate in total chaos and functional dysfunction rather than move and risk being uncomfortable. I stayed in an abusive marriage because of comfort! Yes, it was abusive, but I was comfortable in the midst of the mess. I knew what to expect from the ex! And when we know what to expect, that makes us comfortable. But check this out, comfort is also rooted in fear. So even though I knew what to expect, I was still afraid. I was afraid -not so much to leave my marriage, but more so afraid of what others would think of me leaving. So instead of risking the gossip and judgment of others, I stayed comfortable. I was also comfortable with the financial life he provided because, hell, after all he was making over six figures. At the time I was afraid that I could not support myself if I left. So, I settled for comfort. Because of comfort, I spent many days very unhappy! I wasted so many years of my life that I cannot get back! Man... F! Comfort! I now live beyond the boundaries of comfort! I refuse to let the fear of being uncomfortable keep me settled for less than I deserve or want! My Beloved it's time to step out of the comfort zone! Putting ourselves in uncomfortable situations is essential to growth. What have you been wanting to do or say but you've allowed comfort to hold you back? Everything we want, and need is right outside its boundaries. Now of course I don't expect us to go from 0 to 10 in one step however, we must take steps even if that means going from 0 to 1. It's the movement that matters. And each time we step, it become a little easier to move. Don't let comfort stop you from becoming the best you! So... say it with me! And say it loudly!! "F! Comfort!" AGAIN! "F! Comfort!!!! I don't fear you! I fear living life never having done something that I really want to do!" Now that that's out of your way, GO DO IT!!

When You Need To Feel Acceptance

Morning Cup of F! That! with Coffee...
Thank You, Jesus, for loving me and accepting me just as I am! It's hard enough these days trying to be yourself. And it's sho'nuff hard trying to be something we're not or trying to fit in to someone else's ideal image of us. I did that for a few years and let me tell you I suffered immensely, almost to the point of death. I tried to be "his" everything and fit into "his" ideal image. I changed so much so that I did not to even recognize myself anymore. And all of this for the sake of what I thought was love. Man ...was I clearly mistaken! I had no clue of what real love was. And that's what happens when we live for the love and acceptance of man and not God. Nevertheless, I learned a valuable lesson about love and acceptance. Thank God I did! Once I realized the error of my ways, He healed my broken spirit and showed me what real love is, what it looks like

and how it feels. I'm so thankful that God loves and accepts me for who I am! When we live for His love and acceptance, everything else will line up accordingly. My Beloved, F! living for the love and acceptance of man! That -ish can change from day to day anyway! And although, "Living for the Love of You" it's a great song, the Isley Brothers had it alllllll wrong! We should be living for the love of God; which is unconditional and never changing! He's waiting with open arms to love and accept us just as we are. If He did it for me, I know He'll do it for YOU! Once we completely receive and embody the love and acceptance of The Divine One, we won't feel the need to seek that love and acceptance from others. It won't matter because we will already know that we're loved and accepted! Additionally, we will be able to give that love and acceptance to others freely! If you didn't know ...you gonna learn TODAY!

When You Want To Try Something New

Morning Cup of F! That! with Coffee...
I'm not afraid to step outside my "comfort zone" to try something new! For years, I have worn my hair pretty much in the same short style because I like it! It makes me feel comfortable. However, every now and then, I change it up a bit but I always come back to my short hair style because I think short hair rocks! We like what we like and that's great however, it's also exciting to push the envelope and dare to do something different! We get use to the same things, go the same places, eat the same foods and so on. And because we do the same ole familiar things all the time, we end up missing out on all that life has to offer. Trying something new can be a shock to our system but in a good way! And besides, how will we know if we don't step outside our comfort zone and try something new! My Beloved today is the day to step outside your box and try something new! Let's enjoy all the pleasures that life has to offer! Let's live without any regrets! And even if we go back to doing the same ole familiar things that we enjoy and are comfortable with, at least we tried something new! F! That, I refuse to look up years from now and say I would've, should've, could've when I can right now! I'm going to try something new TODAY and so should YOU!

When You Need To Speak Up For Yourself

Morning Cup of F! That! with Coffee..
I'm so grateful that I learned how to speak up for myself! Growing up I was terribly shy. It was challenging for me to make friends because I was too scared to speak up. I didn't really speak up in classes a lot either,

because I didn't want the attention on me. It wasn't until I went to college that I started speaking up because I really didn't have a choice. When I went to Alabama State University, I didn't know a single person in the entire state of Alabama -until my god sister Yolanda moved back a few months later- so I had to learn quickly how to speak up and advocate for myself! Even then I didn't always speak up like I should have. As a result, I missed out on opportunities and experiences. Things happened that, could have been avoided, all because I didn't speak up. My Beloved, we have got to speak up! Stop going through life pissed off, angry and complaining all because you missed out on opportunities and experiences! It's your fault because you failed to speak up! We fail to tell our partner(s) what we need. We fail to talk to our boss about that promotion or that problem at work. We fail to talk with those who could evoke change. How will anyone know what we want or need if we don't speak up? If we want to be heard, we have to make some noise! However, here's the secret, speaking up does not mean "popping off" "snapping" being rude or nasty. That's not effective! Nor, does speaking up mean getting behind a keyboard and posting on social media. That keyboard courage is just passive aggressive -ish that floats off into cyberspace. Speaking up involves having a purposeful conversation, yup actually talking - not texting or posting on social media hoping "they" will see your status update! F! staying quiet! I want my voice to be heard. I want y'all to know what I need and what I want. It might not always be easy but it's necessary! It's the only way to have your voice heard. Speak up today! Tell someone what you want or need!

When You Need Inspiration

Morning Cup of F! That! with Coffee ...
Inspiration is the stuff that dreams are made of! It's that thing that keeps us going when we feel like giving up. It's motivation! It's moves us to creativity. It's that act right that keeps us acting right! However because life happens, we sometimes lose our inspiration. When we do, our spark goes out. We lose meaning and we begin to slowly wither away. Life becomes monotonous, dull and depressing. But here's the secret My Beloved, we don't have to lose our inspiration because it's all around us! Our spirits just have to remain open. When we truly open our hearts and minds, inspiration will find us when we least expect it! That connection between spirit and energy is all is takes to set fire to the flame of inspiration. And when it does...life begins again! Thank God I've become reacquainted with inspiration because that other -ish was meaningless! And besides, F that! Life is to short not to Live Inspired Feel Empowered! I'm inspired so I can inspire!

When You Need To Stop Wasting Time

Morning Cup of F! That! with Coffee...
I'm so grateful that I have learned to stop wasting time and energy focusing on people, things and situations that really don't matter...because the one thing that's for damn sure is that life is not promised! F*ck tomorrow, you better honor each moment and opportunity! Start spending more time with and focusing on people that truly love you, things that are positive and situations that build you! Oh, and save the bull -ish tired ass excuses! Because the moment something happens, we wanna start slanging snot and crying about how much we loved them and how much they meant! Or we want to act like that person, situation or thing was super important to us!! Save it! If your loved ones, things, situations really matter, tell them TODAY!! Show it NOW!! Waiting until our loved one is casket sharp and/ or situations and things are destroy is useless! Real fact and gut check...you don't have the rest of your life to make it right, so put this book down right now and take that opportunity NOW...I love you!!

When You Need To Be Reminded That Everything Don't Apply To Everybody

Morning Cup of F! That! with Coffee ...
Thank You, Jesus, I've learned that some things just don't apply to certain situations - at least not in its entirety. I was having a conversation with my bestie the other day and as we were chatting some things became very clear. And as our conversation continued, I realized that some of my "truths" or "beliefs" that I stood firmly on or held as non-negotiable may actually have been creating unnecessary challenges for me. We create these standards and/or boundaries that help to govern our relationships with others. And anything that falls outside these particular standards and/or boundaries or when we feel that people aren't upholding them, we sometimes tend to create situations that really do not exist. And now we're all in our head trying to figure this -ish out! Here's the thing though...our standards and/or boundaries sometimes fail to account for factors that other people cannot control. Meaning that individuals may have the best and truest intentions however, when things happen beyond their control, we cannot tax them for it. There's too many variables, in life, over which we do not have any control. It's unfair not to give folks a chance or the benefit of the doubt based on something that is out of THEIR control. So, by the end of the conversation, even though in the beginning I was like F! that, I had to pull

my -ish together because I knew my bestie was right! My Beloved, who and/or what are you unnecessarily taxing? Each situation and/or person is different. We can't hold folks accountable to a one size fits all standard or boundary. It just doesn't work that way! Just like one size fits all outfits clearly don't fit everyone. Now look, I am NOT saying dismiss your standards or drop your boundaries. I am saying that we have to learn to be more discerning and understanding with how we apply them. Ease up a bit on some things, people, and situations. Let's stop creating unnecessary situations and challenges for ourselves. Everybody is not out to hurt us. People can only do what THEY can do. They cannot control other people or situations. At best, they can respond accordingly within the context, guideline or framework they've been given. So sometimes, they may mean easing up on that someone and cutting them a little slack for doing the best they can, given the situation. At the end of the day, if that person is sincere and genuinely trying and making an effort, you gotta give them credit for that. However, if that changes then you gotta call'em out, cut'em off, and cut'em loose! Thanks, bestie! See... "when you ain't looking, I be listening!"

When You Need To Appreciate The NOW

Morning Cup of F! That! with Coffee ...
Thank You, Jesus, for reminding me of the importance of living in and appreciating the NOW! I've said so many times that I wish I had...or I should've have... I've even said I can't wait until...or I'm so looking forward to... I was so busy either looking back or so far ahead that I was not living in or appreciating the moment. When we spend too much time look behind we cannot see where we're going and when we spend so much time looking forward, we lose focus on what's right in front of us. We spend the majority of our lives in the past or in the future. When we reside in either of those spaces, we are unable to experience the beauty of the now! We're unable to see, taste, touch, hear and live life the fullest because we're wrapped up in two dimensions the do not exist. The past does not exist because well, it's the past. It's over. And because we have not arrived in the future, we cannot fully participate in that which does not exist. So now we reside in this weird and uncomfortable state of existence that we've created for ourselves. F! That! I'm tired of missing special moments, opportunities and experiences because I'm not living in the now. My Beloved, where are you? Are you still in the past or so far in the future that you cannot experience the now. We can't beat ourselves up for what did or didn't happen in our past and we certainly can't spend life worrying about what's going to happen in the future. Now of course I'm not saying don't appreciate the past or don't look forward to and plan for the future. I am, however, saying don't forget to live NOW!

When You're Procrastinating

Morning Cup of F! That! with Coffee ...

Thank You, Jesus, that I've gotten so much better at not procrastinating. If you're like me, then sometimes you procrastinate. Every now and then, I will put something off and wait until the very last minute to get it done, especially if it's something that I really don't have an interest in doing. And sometimes, I even make myself feel better by saying: "I work best under pressure." Man... that right there is a bunch of "make me feel good" BS! LOL Now while I do work very well under pressure, and I've created some of my best work under pressure, I still have to be honest with myself and call it what it is...procrastination! There! I said it! pro-cras-ti-nation! Whew! Admitting is the first step! Now on to the awakening! When we procrastinate, we put off the inevitable, only to have to face it much later; and much later is usually much worse. Although procrastination can be a beautiful distraction, it can also be our worst enemy! It prevents us from moving forward, doing what we need to do, and handling our business! It's also an enabler! It's a barrier to our success! Procrastination allows us to hide behind a whole bunch of bull -ish we call excuses, reasons, justifications, or whatever other clever name we can come up with! And while procrastination may indeed fuel some of our best work, it creates unnecessary stress, burn out, frustration, depression, other health issues, and so much more. When procrastinating backs, us into a corner, our claws come out and attitudes begin to flare. But the fact of the matter is, we don't have anyone to blame but ourselves! So why continue to do this to ourselves? Why continue to invite this kind of unnecessary distress into our lives? My Beloved, it's time to face procrastination! It's time to set realistic smart goals, objectives, and deadlines, and create schedules or "to-do" lists. Not only will this help keep us on track, but it will also help us see and celebrate incremental success! Yes, this may feel unnatural at first, and it will definitely take some self-control, but in order to beat procrastination, we must implement some tools and strategies that work for us. So TODAY, think about something that you've been wanting and waiting to do, but for whatever reason you just keep putting it off! It doesn't have to be anything major, just DO it! F! procrastination! Let's stop waiting until tomorrow because guess what? Tomorrow may never come! The time is now! Do it NOW!! Like RIGHT NOW! What are you waiting for? I mean...go'on!!

When You Need To Slow Down

Morning Cup of F! That! with Coffee ...

Today I'm so grateful that I've learned to slow down. I used to have a habit of rushing. Rushing to get to my destination, or trying to finish an assignment quickly, and even rushing into relationships. But what I realized is that when I was rushing, I missed out on important details and made plenty of mistakes I might not have made if I would've just slowed down and took my time. At times, I've even put my life in danger because I was rushing. Thank God I've learned that rushing and trying to do things quickly was not worth my life nor the opportunities that I missed out on by rushing. I now take my time appreciating everything along the way. My Beloved, are you in the habit of rushing through life? If so, it's time to slow down. It will be there when we get there. If not, then it wasn't meant for us. So, if it means we have to plan better, leave a little earlier and/or take more time getting to know someone, then that's what we have to do. In the end, the extra time we take will help to reduce stress and increase the quality of our life. So, let's make it a priority today to slow down, stop, and appreciate the roses! Aren't they beautiful?!

When You Need To Learn To Embrace The Pain

Morning Cup of F! That! with Coffee ...
Thank You, Jesus, for the pain! Pain is a debilitating feeling that keeps us immobile, causes us great distress, discomfort, and agony, not to mention, it hurts like hell! We never want to experience pain. However, pain is so necessary. I'm so grateful for every tear I've cried into a puddle for myself! I'm so grateful for every time I collected my scattered and shattered broken heart! I'm thankful for the heartaches that cut like shards of glass; bleeding intensely with a myriad of uncertain emotions! Thank you for every time I fell and had to get back up and dust myself off, and for all the "no's" that resonated in the chambers of my heart accompanied by the sting of emptiness, I bow in eternal gratefulness! For I have walked in dark places of misery, held hands with sorrow, and came face-to-face with desperation! It was all a Divine lesson with opportunity for growth! I was also reminded that no matter how painful it is...God is able! I think of all the times He has brought me through! I might have been worn out, tattered, and torn, but I survived all because of His mercy! Without the pain, I would not be who I am today! Because of the pain, I am a much better woman, a stronger woman! My Beloved, F! That! Don't run from the pain! It's inevitable! It's part of life. When you begin to feel that pain, put your big girl panties on or your big boy drawers on and go toe-to-toe with it! We must learn to embrace pain and move through it. And sometimes we may have to fight our way through and that's ok! But when we come out on the other side ...My God! Oh, please trust and believe I know that it's not easy! But without ever experiencing pain, we will not truly know the beauty of pleasure! We cannot authentically celebrate what feels good! And doggone, I feel soooo good! Life feels soooo good! Did I say so good? Yup, I did!

When You Need To Pray

Morning Cup of F! That! with Coffee ...

Thank You, Jesus, that I've learned to pray! When I was about 4 or 5 years old, my mother taught me the Lord's Prayer. Every night before I would go to bed, we would kneel beside the bed and I would repeat The Prayer after her. Over the years, I learned to develop my own prayer relationship with God. I learned how important prayer was in my life! More importantly, I learned not to ask just anybody and everybody to pray for me! Man... F! that! Everyone out there praying for us, is not praying for our success, health, and wealth! There are many people out there praying--secretly and even openly--for our demise. Mean-spirited, hateful, unhappy, scorned, people actually set out to prey on us, befriend us to betray us, and try to destroy us. Now why is that? Other people's perception of who we are or what we have can be very distorted and based in fantasy. Nevertheless, because of their perception, they form some unrealistic ideal of us, which creates feelings of envy, jealously, hate, etc. and so they seek and attack. The truly unfortunate thing is that sometimes we can be blinded because these people take the shape of our family members, close friends, co-workers and even our partners. Yup, I said it! Therefore, it is extremely important that we learn how to pray for ourselves! My Beloved, have you learned how to pray? Seeking prayers and counsel from those not divinely aligned can result in disaster! Remember, everybody is not connected to The Source. The devil hears our prayers too. However, the beautiful thing about it is that when WE are connected to The Source and when WE spend time in prayer, God will take those "prayers" that others meant for our harm and use it for our good! Won't He do it?! So, the next time you ask someone to pray, just remember that your prayers are just as direct and powerful. So... gon' ahead, bow yo' head, and get yo' prayer on!

When You Need To Face The Fire

Morning Cup of F! That! with Coffee ...

God's Fire is an oxidation, reduction, and refining process. During the fire, we are reduced so that we can experience God. Oxidation of all the decay, corrosion and other pollutants begins to breakdown. During refining, we are tested, bent, shaped, and molded until we come forth as pure gold. The fire is a way of bringing us into all of our fullness so that we can become right with God and so that we can continue to fulfill His Will and Purpose for our lives. The fire also prepares us for receiving all that God has for us! But before we can receive it, we must be proven by Grace under fire. My Beloved just know that whatever you're going through is a test! God is preparing us for something much greater than we are right now, but first we have to go through the fire. So, when you're ready to give up, just remember it's a test! It's only a test! And when the fire gets too hot and the flames are glaring high and burning fast, just remember what we learned in grade school--stop, drop and roll. Stop and listen to that small inner voice. Drop into position and get ready to roll into all that God has for you!

When You Need To Be Grateful For The Frogs

Morning Cup of F! That! with Coffee ...
Today, I am so grateful for all the "frogs" that I've kissed! Because of you all, I am that much closer to my prince. Like many, I have loved and lost! Each love was true and real, adding and even sometimes taking away something very significant from my life. I look upon each experience with admiration and no regrets, for each opened many doors and expanded my horizons; teaching me what I need as well as want in a relationship. But most of all, I learned I cannot change anyone except myself. Frogs still hop into my life but thank God I no longer kiss them hoping that they will become something that they're not capable of! My prince will already be a prince when our Divine paths cross! He will already be what I need and want. He will not look to me to complete him because he will already be complete. The kiss will only be confirmation. Until then, I'm not afraid to watch the frogs hop by alone until I get what I deserve!

When You Need To Be Reminded To Live

Morning Cup of F! That! with Coffee...
Thank You, Jesus, I've re-learned what it really means to live! I was watching this video and the gentleman being interviewed in the video was speaking about various topics related to life. One particular topic really caught my attention. It was about death. The interviewer asked him if he was afraid of dying. The man being interviewed so eloquently stated "No, I do not fear death. I embrace it. The knowledge that I'm going to one day die creates the focus for the kind of life that I want to live today." That was extremely powerful! It resonated in my spirit! It helped to put so many things into perspective! My Beloved, we live life as if we're going to live forever. As if we're promised tomorrow. We're not! And no one knows the hour in which we shall depart from this life. We waste soooo much time on things, people, places, jobs, situations, etc. that are irrelevant! And for what? Man...F! That! I don't want to live like that! I want to live with a sense of urgency! I don't want to waste my time left on this Earth waiting for tomorrow. It may never come. And I'm also not going to live my life in a box or being who others think I should be! I'm going to live

unapologetically and authentically - whatever that is for me!!! I don't know when my time will come, but I absolutely refuse to waste what's left! I'm going to live, laugh and leave a lasting legacy that will score a victory for humanity! I will not die ashamed of never living the life that I wanted to live! So, when you see me living it up, join in or please step aside and continue to wait for your tomorrow...

When You Need To Be Reminded That There's No Need To Compete

Morning Cup of F! That! with Coffee ...

I'm so grateful that I don't feel the need to compete! I have never been a competitive type chick! I never understood the need to nor have I had the desire to measure my worth, value, ability or self-esteem against someone or something else. I never saw the point. I never felt that I had to beat someone in a game, sports or anything. To get all aggressive and caught up in losing or wining is just not me. And beside what I've learned over the years is that no matter whether we win or lose, in the end we will still receive what's meant to be ours. I don't believe that anyone can take what's meant for me! I don't believe that anyone can have my spot! What God has for me is authentically mines! Just like what He has for you is authentically yours! So... why compete? We are individually gifted! If we spent time focusing on and cultivating that, we'd be surprised at what could be accomplished. When we are so focused on competing and proving ourselves to others, we lose sight of our gift, purpose, and passion. We lose sight of ourselves because we measure ourselves by unrealistic expectations, standards, abilities and the focus of others; which we can never measure up to. And so now we live life believing we're somehow a failure or a loser. Man... please!! My Beloved, F! competition! Don't tie your worth, value, gift, ability or self-esteem to competing! At some point in life, we all win some and lose some. So? It doesn't matter how good someone else is. It doesn't matter what someone else has. They are not our competition! God has designed each and every one of us with our own brand and unique purpose. NO ONE can do what we have been created to do, even if it appears to be similar (or even if we do the exact same thing). Don't believe the hype! Competition is what's keeping us apart and killing us! Ingest, digest, and absorb that part!

When You Need To Take Action

Morning Cup of F! That! with Coffee ...

Thank You, Jesus, for the call to action! Action can be defined as the process of getting something done. It's moving--with purpose--to accomplish something we desire! It's stepping out on faith and believing the impossible and seeing the invisible. So often we complain and gripe about things, but we fail to move in faith to take action. We do not actually take the steps to creating or providing solutions to the challenges that we complain about. So, what's the point of complaining? Ya know, it's one thing to sit back and talk about what needs to or should be done. But it's another thing to get up off our butt and out of our comfort zone and move into action. If we don't take action, we don't see results! We don't see change! Action is just like faith, without works it's dead! So, what does action look like? Action is offering a creative solution to a problem, creating a plan to accomplish it and then actively putting the plan into works. It's getting out here in these streets and making some noise. It's standing up and fighting for what you believe in regardless of what society, family or friends say; even if you have to stand alone! It's offering a helping hand to those who are out there actually doing the work. It's modeling the change or action that you want to see. Here's what action is NOT. Action is not expecting others to do it and complaining when they don't or if they don't do it your way. It's not sitting at your computer posting status updates about how things need to change. It's not blocking or hating on the efforts of others that are out here doing the work. It's not sitting around "the table" talking cute and coming up with great ideals that never materialize. My Beloved, we need to be about that action! What do you need to take action on right now? What are you going to do about it? I'm calling you out! I'm calling you to action! For everything you've ever complained about or wanted to change, here's your opportunity! Take at least one action step towards addressing it TODAY! Just one! That's a beautiful start! F! waiting on someone else to take action! Kick fear to the side and step over comfort! It's time to move something!!

When You Need To Break The Cycle

Morning Cup of F! That with Coffee ...

Thank You, Jesus, for helping me to break the cycle! Grandma and them" and "momma and them" will have you all F -ed up! They had a way of doing things that worked for them. Over the years, they passed down these intergenerational patterns, thoughts, beliefs and behaviors to us. Some of these things were very helpful or healthy while others were, well...not so much! And it's the "not so much" that is harmful to us. The interesting part about all of this is that we never questioned grandma, momma, or them about why they did what they did. We've just accepted what was passed down as gospel! And most of the time, we just continued on in the same vein - good or bad- as grandma, momma and them without even knowing and understanding why. The only answer we have to explain our thoughts, beliefs, and behaviors is...that's how I was raised. But is that good enough? Our failure to ask questions or challenge these intergenerational patterns, thoughts, beliefs and/or behaviors leaves us without a true sense of self; which is essential for our identity and sense of authenticity. What worked for grandma, momma and them, may not work for us! When we were kids, we did not have a choice but as adults we most certainly do! My Beloved, it's time to break the cycle! It's time to create your own path! It's time to do what works for you! F! sticking to those old antiquated intergenerational patterns, thoughts, beliefs and behaviors! I absolutely refuse to stay in bondage and repeat the negative, unhealthy cycle and continue to fail generation after generation! It begins with us! So, shall I pass you a hammer? 1,2,3 break that cycle!!

When You Need To Be Thankful For Your Mistakes

Morning Cup of F! That! with Coffee ...
Thank You, Jesus, for my mistakes! There's a misconception that making mistakes makes us stupid or weak. Society has taught us that if we make a mistake, we should feel bad or just fade into the abyss of embarrassment. Our ego, pride, and fear are the culprits that feed us this lie. However, the truth is that making mistakes actually brings us one step closer to our goals. How you might ask? Well, if we don't make mistakes, then we don't learn. We don't grow! Mistakes are essential to growth! Each and every person on this Earth has made mistakes at some point in their lives. You and I, My Beloved, aren't exempt! It's time to put the big girl panties and big boy drawers on and own up to our mistakes! We must acknowledge that we've made a mistake. The blame game, deflecting and ignoring does not get us anywhere but in the fast lane of denial - which by the way is not helpful for anyone. Once we've acknowledged and taken ownership, look at the lesson. What should we have learned from the mistake? What could we have done differently? How will we avoid this in the future? Finally, let it go and move on! Don't linger in the midst of the mistake! For crying out loud, we're human. To err is the human way! But instead of sulking in it, pick yourself up, dust off and keep it moving! F! ego, pride, and fear! They will have you caught up every time. If you're making mistakes then congratulations, you're doing it right! You're making progress! You're living! Never let a mistake or even multiple mistakes keep you from opportunities. Admit the mistake to yourself or whoever and keep moving on to greatness! Say it

with me...mistakes are for the successful! Next time you say it, you gotta really believe it! Say it again! Say it loud! MISTAKES ARE FOR THE SUCCESSFUL!

When You Need To Find The Strength To Dig Deep

Morning Cup of F! That! with Coffee...
Thank You, Jesus, for showing me how to dig deep! We all have to work through many layers of ourselves to get to the root cause of our stuff. However, instead of digging deep, most of us just stop at the superficial/ outer layer. You know the one where we try to make others and ourselves believe that we have it all together. Occasionally, we go to the inner layer where we may acknowledge something to ourselves but do nothing about it. Rarely, if ever, do we go to the root layer- cause of our -ish- because it requires us to dig deep. When we dig that deep, we have to face our -ish? That's tough! But if we really want to make significant changes or grow, then we have to put in the work and dig deep! There's no easy way around it. My Beloved, it's time to get knee deep in it! It's time to start digging deep! Grab your shovel, put your boots on and start digging up your -ish! It may take some time, but it will be well worth it! My favorite dessert of all time is a chocolate molten lava cake! Yummmmmmmy! A chocolate molten lava cake is a dome-shaped chocolate cake that is topped with confectioners' sugar and filled with hot melted chocolate on the inside. When you look at the cake, it looks beautiful! It's well put together! It's served with strawberries, ice cream, chocolate drizzle, small chocolate beads and mint leaves. However it's not until you scrap the surface, break through the outer layer and dig deeper that the "good stuff," the melted chocolate comes oozing out! You see the melted chocolate doesn't come out right away and it won't unless you dig deep! F! the confectioners' sugar and the cake! I don't want just the surface sugar and outer layer of cake! I want the good stuff! I want the molten lava! In order to get to it, I have to put in the work and dig deep! When I do, it's soooo worth it and it taste so damn good!

When You Need To Ask Questions

Morning Cup of F! That! with Coffee ...
Children are curious by nature. That's how we learn and grow. When I was younger, I was always asking what, when, where, why and how? I always wanted to know the answers. I always wanted to gain an understanding. Actually, my natural curiosity led me into the field of sexuality. Even though I asked questions, and most of the time got answers, at the end of the day

what my parents said was it! As children, we grow up with our parents or other adult's morals, values, beliefs, thoughts, attitudes, etc. We are taught and expected to just accept things as they are because an adult said so. However, as we begin to grow into ourselves, we must begin to question everything! What worked for us or what was taught to us as children may not fit our lives as adults. Society frowns upon questioning. Society has turned the act of questioning into some form of defiance, disrespect, or aggressive challenging behavior. If someone ask a question, we get annoyed, irritated, in some cases try to belittle or destroy the person asking the question or we simply just don't address it at all. As a result of not asking the question, we believe everything we see and hear as real. What's even more crazy is that oftentimes these societal beliefs, attitudes, behaviors, values, intergenerational patterns etc. may not work for us but because it's all we know and/or because we're comfortable, we just accept it and settle without ever asking a single question. My Beloved! We have to ask the questions no matter how tough it may be. Questions help us gain understanding and clarity! Questions help to solidify and justify why we believe what we believe. It lends credence to our very existence. In addition, asking questions challenges the status quo. It takes us out of the box and creates a unique space for our lives. Asking questions gives us knowledge and power! That's what society doesn't want because when you're called out. you're forced to face your ish! Who really wants to do that? F! That! I'm asking the questions- unapologetically! When it comes to my life, I'm questioning everything because everything is not always what it seems. You can't just say something and expect me to go along with it. I'm way to grown to not be able to ask the questions that I need the answer to. So, if I ever give you some push back on something that you say, it's not disrespect or defiance, I'm just trying to understand more about life.

When You Need To Be Reminded About The Power Of Words

Morning Cup of F! That! with Coffee ...
Thank You, Jesus, that I understand the power of words! Nothing convinced me of exactly how true this was until I died a thousand times from the words of my ex-husband! This man's words would cut like shard glass, sting like a scorpion, and stab with hurt and pain. His words were so piercing, that over time I actually began to believe all the vile words he said to me and about me. It was during that marriage that I really embodied the phrase "death and life are in the power of the tongue." Man...words are like speeding bullets; once they come out, they cannot be taken back! The damage is already done! And even though you may apologize, the words still leave footprints forever embedded in a person's heart, and apologies become empty like hollow hearts. Unfortunately, often times we just talk

without regards to what comes out of our mouths. We say things because we're upset, angry, hurt, or in the midst of an argument/disagreement without regards to the potential damage or lasting impact it may have on our lives, others' lives, and our relationships. We seem to forget or not acknowledge that words hurt just as much, if not more, than physical pain; leaving lasting scars that can be difficult to heal. Words are very powerful! The words we speak (positive or negative) are manifested in our lives. They become us, and even those around us. This is why I try to choose my words very carefully. My Beloved, like the old folks used to tell us when we were kids, "watch yo' mouth!" F! That! It's not acceptable to pop off and say whatever you want to say in the heat of the moment, especially to those you say you love! We are in control of the words we choose to speak! So...what words will you choose today? What will you speak into your life? Let us pray that we always learn to think before we speak, choose our words wisely, choose words that are life-giving and that our tongues always speak with grace (and love), seasoned with salt, that we may know how we ought to answer everyone. TODAY, I speak Divine blessings and supernatural Favor over our lives!

When You Need To Appreciate The Special Moments

Morning Cup of F! That! with Coffee ...
Thank You, Jesus for special moments! We honor and celebrate birthdays, weddings, graduations, anniversaries, holidays, etc. because of their significance to us; because they're special moments. But how often do we honor and celebrate the DAILY shared moments that we have with our loved ones i.e. a date, exchange of loving words, warm embrace, look in his/her eyes, a text a phone call, etc. These moments are just as special and should not be taken lightly or for granted. Anytime we share a moment with a loved one, we should be appreciative and cherish it! For it is a moment in time unlike any other that we cannot get back, so let's not waste it! My Beloved let's make each moment special! The fact that we are still alive and able to share and spend time with our loved ones is reason enough! Let's use TODAY to make sure that we let someone know just how truly special the moments that we share or have shared with them are. Stop waiting until they're casket sharp to honor and celebrate them! Carpe diem! You never know if or when the opportunity will come again. Don't let it pass you by TODAY! F! That! I'm living in our moment(s)! I'm honoring and celebrating now! I'm taking every opportunity I can because I need you to know that EVERY SINGLE moment is authentic! It's real! It's special!

When You Finally Realize Just How Beautiful Your Love Is

Thank, You Jesus! I've learned that my love is too beautiful to be manipulated and used against me! We must stop believing that just because people accept things from us, or allow us to do things for them, that it means that they love us because it does not! All it means is that they are selfish, inconsiderate, and disrespectful, and willing to sit back and allow us to do whatever they need or want us to do. They are willing to take from us as long as we are willing to give. That's not love and acceptance! That's someone benefiting off our generosity and kind heart! That's someone willing to take advantage of our love for them and desire to be loved by them. Here's a tough fact for us to face: no matter what we do, how much we inconvenience ourselves, or how much money we spend, some people are just not capable and/or willing to love us the way we need to be loved. Here's an even tougher fact: not only are they incapable or not willing to love us, but the minute we stop doing stuff and being there for them, they have the unmitigated gall to get mad and try to make us feel bad. Aaaand to add insult to injury, they threaten to stop "loving us! What kind of bull -ish is that?!! But because of our desire to be loved by them and our desire to prove how much we love them, we put up with this foolishness. We even convince ourselves that they're acting like that because they really do love and need us. Well, here's a gut check...that's NOT love! It may be *need*, but definitely not love! It is control and manipulation at its best! It's someone playing with our emotions and using it for their benefit. My Beloved, it's time to stop looking for love from the wrong people! This includes spouses, partners, significant others, parents, friends, or whatever the hell you call them!! Stop letting people play on our desire to be loved and accepted! Continuing to seek something from someone who's not capable or willing to give -for whatever reason is absolutely *insane*! There comes a time in our life when we have to say F! That! and walk away! Yes, it may not be easy but it's damn sure worth it! Because when we do, we open up the door to a beautiful world of people who are willing to love and accept us as we are! We create a space that allows our perfect love to come in- the love that we've always wanted, the love that will love us back! So ask yourself the tough questions today! How much longer am I willing to settle for less than I deserve? How much longer will I allow people to use me? How much more time am I willing to waste trying to make selfish people love me? How much longer am I willing to live my live without the love I really want and desire?" Once you get your answers, make your moves because they do not deserve you!!! Life is waaaaaaaay to short not to have the love you desire! Say it with me...."my love is too beautiful to {insert your words here}!

When You Need To Say F! That!

Morning Cup of F! That! with Coffee ...

A lot of people have asked me what this whole "Morning Cup of F! That! with Coffee" thing is all about. My answer is very simple! It's about me! Nope that's not selfish either, it's self-preservation! It's a celebration of self-love! It comes from a place of genuine authenticity, vulnerability and transparency! Man... I have been through soooo many things in my life that I have allowed them to hold me back. I have allowed soooo many people, especially those close to me, to stand in the way and prevent me from doing things that I really loved or wanted to do all because of their fear, disagreement, lack of understanding and/or discomfort. In doing all of this, I lost me. I was depressed! I was unhappy! I was broken! I was fighting! Fighting for the right to be! Fighting for the right to breathe! Fight for the right to feel my heartbeat! Fighting for the right to live my life! MY LIFE! In the process, I died! Now that I am on the other side of things, I have learned that being who I am regardless of what others think, feel, do, believe, decide, etc. is not only important it's essential! It's the only way to live! I cannot be there for anyone, if I can't present and show up as ME-whatever that is for ME! That's all I got y'all! If you can't feel me or understand me, then F! That! That's your -ish to deal with! My worth, my life is too beautiful to be suffocated to death! So, when I say F! That, I MEAN That! No disrespect intended. I'm just unapologetically ME! My Beloved, everyone will always have something to say, from now until forever! You gotta be bold enough, fearless enough and a little crazy enough to say...F! THAT! Naw, it's not rude or disrespectful, it's just being authentic and unapologetically honoring you! They, them, and the others will catch on later. If not, then F! That! Don't die for they, them and the others! LIVE for you!!! YES, LIVE FOR YOU!!! Any questions...

APPENDIX B
SMART GOALS

The SMART goal criteria is a goal-setting technique that moves beyond the realm of basic goal-setting into an action plan of movement and results. The SMART acronym itself has several different variations, but I find the terms below to be some of the most purposeful when setting goals.

Specific. Your goal should be specific. A specific goal has a much greater chance of being accomplished than a general goal. To set a specific goal, you must answer the five "W" questions: who, what, when, where, why. **S** can also stand for sincere. A goal is something that is near and dear to your heart. Something that you have identified as something you want to accomplish for yourself and not anyone else.

Measurable. Establish concrete criteria for measuring progress toward the attainment of each goal you set. When you measure your progress, you stay on track, reach your target dates, and experience the joy of achievement that motivates you to continue efforts required to reach more goals.
Motivational. Goals need to be motivational. They need to inspire you to take action and make progress. One of the best ways to make goals motivational is to ask yourself why you want to achieve it.
Meaningful. Your goals should be meaningful to you. This just helps to ensure that they are really your goals rather than your significant others', friends', parents', society's goals.

Attainable/**A**chievable. Goals must achievable. The best goals require you to stretch a bit to achieve them but are not impossible to achieve. When you identify goals that are most important to you, you begin to figure out ways you can make them come true. Make sure that you have the abilities, skills, and financial capacity to reach them. Attitude also plays a huge factor in attaining your goals.

Realistic. To be realistic, a goal must represent an objective that you are both willing and able to work toward.
Relevant - Good goals are relevant to you and to your life. Relevant goals are meaningful and significant; they can make a difference in your life. If a goal is not relevant to you, then you need to ask yourself why you are even contemplating it.

A goal should be grounded within a time frame. With no time frame tied to it, there's no sense of urgency.

T can also stand for Tangible – A goal is tangible when you can experience it with one of the senses, that is taste, touch, smell, see, or hear. When your goal is tangible, you have a better chance of making it specific and measurable and thus attainable.

Examples of SMART Goal:

• Example of a basic goal: "I want to lose weight."

• Example of a SMART goal: "I want to lose 20 pounds by December 15, 2018. I will perform a half hour of cardio and half hour of strength training per day, 5 times a week, and I will limit my carbohydrates and sweet intake to 3 times a week."

Movement: Losing 20 pounds by December 15, 2018.

Action: I will perform a half hour of cardio and half hour of strength training per day, 5 times a week, and I will limit my carbohydrates and sweet intake to 3 times a week."

Activities: To complete my cardio, I will go to dance class twice a week and walk on my treadmill or outside three times a week. I will complete my strength training at home using my body resistance exercises and free weights.

Setting SMART goals are crucial to your success. Once you have a SMART Goal clearly defined, you need to come up with a plan of action for movement! Goals won't magically happen just because you've written them down. Even if you come up with a fantastic SMART goal, you still need to act on it consistently by outlining activities that will help you accomplish your goal.

Doran, George T. "There's a S.M.A.R.T. way to write management's goals and objectives." Management Review 70.11 (Nov. 1981): 35. Business Source Corporate. EBSCO.

ABOUT THE AUTHOR

At age 13, Dr. TaMara Griffin told her mother that she wanted to be a sex therapist! Her passion is deeply rooted in providing individuals with the knowledge, tools, and skills needed to embrace their sexuality. Dr. TaMara is a certified clinical sexologist, sex therapist, author, speaker and radio host with more than 20 years experience speaking, writing and teaching about human sexuality. Dr. TaMara travels the country speaking, consulting and providing extensive trainings to individuals, colleges, universities, business and other organizations about healthy sexuality. She also works extensive with Bedroom Kandi by Kandi Burruss to provide sexuality training and education to a national based of home party consultants.

Dr. TaMara is the author of several books including: Live Inspired Feel Empowered, I AM Sex! A Comprehensive Guide to Understanding Women's Sexuality and It's Not The Birds And The Bees, It's Sex! How To Talk To Children About Sexuality and V! A love Letter To Every Woman And Girl. Dr. TaMara is also currently the Editor in Chief for *Our Sexuality! Magazine*, the premiere magazine for women's sexuality and sexual health. She is also a freelance writer for many online magazines, social media websites or her personal blog "Live Inspired Feel Empowered." Dr. TaMara has been featured in Ebony Magazine, Essence Magazine, Men's Fitness Magazine, DAME, Courageous Woman Magazine, BlackDoctor.org, sexpert.com, and many more.

Dr. TaMara holds a Doctor of Philosophy (PhD) in Human Sexuality, Doctorate of Human Sexuality (DHS), Master of Social Work degree, Master of Science degree in Education, and a Bachelor of Arts degree in Family Life Education. Dr. TaMara is certified in Clinical Sexology; and also a holds several additional certificates including: Sex Therapy, Clinical Sexology, and Erotology; just to name a few.

Follow Dr. TaMara on all social media @drtamaragriffin. Website: www.drtamaragriffin.com

Made in the USA
Columbia, SC
14 August 2021